*The American
Immigration Collection*

Ukrainians in the United States

WASYL HALICH

Arno Press and *The New York Times*

NEW YORK 1970

Reprint Edition 1970 by Arno Press Inc.

LC# 78-129399
ISBN 0-405-00552-0

The American Immigration Collection—Series II
ISBN for complete set 0-405-00543-1

Manufactured in the United States of America

UKRAINIANS
IN THE UNITED STATES

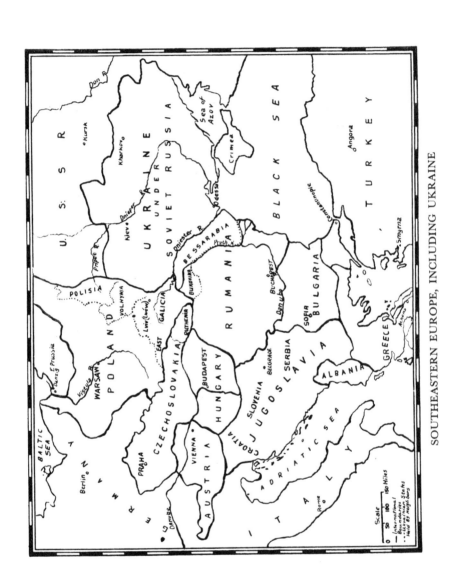

SOUTHEASTERN EUROPE, INCLUDING UKRAINE

UKRAINIANS
IN THE UNITED STATES

By

WASYL HALICH, Ph.D.

THE UNIVERSITY OF CHICAGO PRESS
CHICAGO · ILLINOIS

THE UNIVERSITY OF CHICAGO PRESS · CHICAGO
THE BAKER & TAYLOR COMPANY, NEW YORK; THE CAMBRIDGE UNIVERSITY
PRESS, LONDON; THE MARUZEN-KABUSHIKI-KAISHA, TOKYO, OSAKA,
KYOTO, FUKUOKA, SENDAI; THE COMMERCIAL PRESS, LIMITED, SHANGHAI

To American youth of Ukrainian parentage, often living in two environments and between two cultures, not always cognizant of their racial inheritance or their American opportunities, the author dedicates this volume

PREFACE

DURING the closing decades of the nineteenth century and the years preceding the World War, European immigration to the United States added millions to the ever increasing population. In the main, this was due to overpopulation in several European countries and dissatisfaction with the conditions under which the masses lived. At the same time America offered employment to the unskilled laborers in her growing industries. The Slavic people, to which group the Ukrainians belong, lived under the most adverse conditions in the countries of their birth. Their educational, civic, and religious rights were very limited, and the economic opportunity to improve themselves was almost nonexistent. Therefore, when the masses learned of the opportunities America offered them, they emigrated in large numbers.

The arrival of the so-called "new immigrants" caused some people, among them a number of publicists, to take an antagonistic attitude toward the foreigners. Some of them, through their writings, were responsible for creating race prejudice. A few scholars, however, studied the problem carefully and presented accounts in which they evaluated the immigrant's contribution to America. In so far as Slavic immigration is concerned, not every group has produced its historian as yet, and the students of immigration have in some way neglected some racial groups. Thus, much still remains for future research in this field of American history.

Together with other Slavic nationalities came the Ukrainians. They constituted a considerable percentage of the "new immigration" and helped to furnish the country with industrial labor. They penetrated the coal-mining districts of Pennsylvania, Ohio, West Virginia, and Illinois; hundreds of them likewise found employment in the iron mines of Minnesota and Michigan. The urban regions, especially metropolitan centers of great industries, have in their midst many thousands of hard-working and thrifty Ukrainians. A small percentage of them became farmers in America.

The presentation of the causes of their emigration, time of emigration, numerical importance, distribution in America, occupations, businesses, professions, and social institutions is the object of this volume. In the search for material, on immigration in general and Ukrainians in particular, the United States immigration documents proved of great value. The Ukrainian American newspapers and almanacs (calendars) are indispensable to the study of Ukrainian groups. Such sources, in Ukrainian, may be found only in their places of publication. But as long as the immigrants themselves are still alive in many cases, much valuable information may be obtained from them directly.

In the preparation of this study the author's obligations are numerous, both to individuals and to institutions. His thanks are due to the editors of the following Ukrainian American publications for permitting him to search their files for material and for making available the necessary office accommodations: *America* (Philadelphia), *Narodna Vola* (Scranton), and *Svoboda* (Jersey City). It is impossible to name here all the individuals who gave assistance to the author, but special thanks are due to Rev. Fr. Alex Prystay for permitting him to read his collection of letters and his "Memoirs" in manuscript; to Miss Mary B. Humphrey, who is in charge of government documents at the State University of Iowa; and to Dr. Harrison J. Thornton of the department of history in the same institution, who first pointed out the significance of the topic and throughout a part of the research gave valuable guidance. The author's greatest debt of gratitude, however, is to Mrs. Margaret M. Halich, whose assistance and inspiration were most valuable in bringing this work to its final form.

TABLE OF CONTENTS

LIST OF ILLUSTRATIONS

Whether one traces his Americanism back three centuries to the Mayflower, or three years to the steerage, is not half so important as whether his Americanism of to-day is real and genuine. No matter on what various crafts we came here, we are all now in the same boat. —CALVIN COOLIDGE in a speech to the American Legion Convention at Omaha, Nebraska, October 6, 1925.

CHAPTER I

INTRODUCTION: HISTORICAL BACKGROUND OF THE UKRAINIAN IMMIGRANTS

GEOGRAPHY OF THE UKRAINE

THE Ukraine extends to the Don River on the east, the Caucasian Mountains and the Black Sea on the south, Rumania and Czecho-Slovakia on the southwest, Poland on the west, and White Russia and Russia on the north.[1]* It embraces 384,996 square miles—an area greater in extent than any country in Europe except Russia.[2]

The chief rivers of the Ukraine are the Dniester, Buh (Bug), Dnieper, and Donetz. The "Father Dnieper" is a national river, commemorated in folk songs and ballads. The largest cities are Kiev (the capital), Odessa, Kharkov, and Lwow. The highest mountains of the Ukraine are the Caucasians on the south and the Carpathians on the southwest. A greater part of the country consists of the rich black-soil steppes.

The nature of the soil and the climate resembles that of the Middle West in the United States. The country is rich in mineral resources, such as mineral waters, mineral wax, oil, coal, iron, manganese, and mercury, and is a principal source of quicksilver in Europe.[3]

Since 1919 the Ukraine has been so divided by her neighbors that about thirty millions of her people exist under the Bolshevik regime, seven millions in Western Ukraine are subject to Poland, over a million in the Ukrainian provinces were taken by Rumania, and about six hundred thousand are in Ruthenia, a part of Czecho-Slovakia. Also more than a million live in the United States and other American countries.[4] The people of the Ukraine belong to the Slavic race and differ greatly from the neighboring Poles and Russians,[5] having their own highly developed language, literature, and cultural institutions.

* The notes are found at the end of each chapter.

1

THE KINGDOM OF KIEV

Although the Ukraine was inhabited in the pre-Christian Era, its people remained in a tribal state until the ninth century (A.D.), when a political union was achieved, its strength resting on the cities. During the reign of Vladimir the Great (980–1015) the old Ukraine achieved its zenith: This ruler united all the provinces and established order; his domain extended from the Volga River on the east to the Sian River on the west.[6] When he embraced Christianity in 988, he outlawed paganism in his realm. Christianity existed in the country before Vladimir's period, but he gave it legal status.[7] The Greek clergy brought not only Christianity to the Ukraine but also Greek civilization. Kiev, the capital, became the intellectual and religious center.[8] In the eleventh century the kingdom of Kiev was strong and prosperous and communicated with the West on equal terms commercially and socially.[9]

THE MONGOLIAN INVASION

The golden period of Ukrainian history came to a tragic end in 1240, when the Mongolians, under the leadership of Batu, captured Kiev and despoiled the country. Within a few years almost the entire Ukraine was conquered by the barbarians, and Slavic leadership was undertaken by the primitive Russians of Moscow.[10] It took the Ukrainian people nearly three hundred years to recover from the effects of the Mongolian invasion. The marauders continued sporadic attacks until the eighteenth century. In its distress the Ukraine was an easy prey to enemies from the north and northwest—Russia, Poland, and Lithuania. These did not suffer so much from the Tartar attacks and, in their strength, pressed forward to the conquest of most of the north-central part of the Ukraine.[11]

THE COSSACK PERIOD

The Ukrainians suffered severely from Polish oppression. The Polish nobles seemed bent upon the enslavement of the conquered people. When the foreign oppression became unbearable, the masses of the Ukrainian people again deserted their homes and moved to the uninhabited steppes of southeastern Ukraine, from which their forefathers had fled before the Tartar and Turkish invasions. They preferred to expose themselves to the occasional danger of a barbarian raid rather than to endure the grinding oppression of the Polish overlords. From this migration developed the Cossack period, described by Baron Haxthausen as one of the most interesting phenomena in the history of the Slavic race.[12] Frontier life developed a hardy type of democratic individualism. Frequent Tartar attacks necessitated constant military preparedness,[13] and an irregular army, the Cossacks, came into existence.[14] It consisted of farmers, hunters, fishermen, and craftsmen. By the seventeenth century the Cossacks were famous throughout Europe. Their headquarters and strongholds were located along the rapids of the Dnieper River, the so-called Zaporozhe; hence the origin of the name "Zaporozhian Cossacks." The government of this army was exceedingly democratic; officials were elected, including the highest *hetman* or *ataman*. In time of war the *ataman* was given dictatorial power.[15] The skill of the Cossacks in fighting the Tartars and Turks during the seventeenth and eighteenth centuries brought the Cossacks victories, wealth, and fame, and foreign nations frequently sought their services.[16] In time, the Cossacks took the offensive against their traditional enemies from the east. They did not wait for the Turks to come up the Dnieper to fight but sailed down the river and attacked Turkish cities along the coast of the Black Sea.[17] Constant raids by the Cossacks on these cities made the sultan at Constantinople uneasy, and he frequently appealed to the Polish ruler for help.

Upon their return to the steppes of southeastern Ukraine during the sixteenth and seventeenth centuries, the Ukrainian people found themselves pursued by tribulation. When a community was established "in God's free country," the nobles came, laid claim to the land, and gradually reduced the people to serfdom. The settlers faced the alternatives of moving on still farther south and east, there to face the danger of the Mongolians, or of making a stand to fight for their freedom. The first of these alternatives was followed for a while, for the nobles maintained a well-

organized private army and could always call upon their home
country to support their case. But eventually the people struck
a blow for their freedom. They appealed to the Cossacks for
support, and the Polish-Ukrainian wars followed, in the years
1625, 1630, and 1648–50.[18]
    The greatest leaders of the Cossacks were Sahaidachny,
Khmelnitzky, Krivonos, Doroshenko, and Mazeppa. The most
outstanding of these was Bohdan Khmelnitzky, and under his
leadership the independence of the Ukraine was achieved, in
1649. For this enterprise the Cossacks made an alliance with the
Tartars and almost completely destroyed the Polish army.[19] For
a short period Poland was at the mercy of the Cossacks. While
the war was on, the people of the Ukraine turned upon the
Polish nobles and the Jews, killing thousands of them. The great
objective was the Ukraine "without a nobleman and without a
serf." The newly won freedom, however, was in danger from
the very beginning because the Polish nobles did not give up
their desire to exploit the Ukraine.

ALLIANCE WITH RUSSIA

    In order to protect Ukrainian independence, Khmelnitzky, by
the Treaty of Pereyaslav in 1654, entered into an offensive-de-
fensive alliance with the ruler of Muscovy, Alexcy Michailovich.
The treaty proved very fatal to the Ukraine and prepared the
way for Russian rule. Even during the lifetime of Khmelnitzky,
Russia began to interfere in Ukrainian affairs, but after his death
her evolving aggressiveness put to an end Ukrainian independence. The Ukrainians tried, with the help of Turkey and Sweden,
to free themselves from the "Russian Bear," but all in vain.[20]

PARTITION OF THE UKRAINE

    A democratic Ukraine in the midst of an aristocratic Poland
and Russia was more than these two states would tolerate. In-
tending to put an end to freedom and democracy, they re-estab-
lished a system of nobility and serfdom and, by the Treaty of
Andrussovo, in 1667, divided the Ukraine, Russia taking the
part east of the Dnieper, Poland that west of that river.[21] Het-

man Doroshenko of the Ukraine immediately recognized the protection of the sultan and appealed for his help.[22] The country became a battleground for many years, but the Ukrainians were gradually deprived of their political, civil, and religious rights.[23] Governmental favorites gained offices and riches. The gentry and the people of the towns became Russians or Poles; but the masses, though reduced to serfdom, remained Ukrainian.

THE TRANSPLANTING OF UKRAINIAN CULTURE

The primitive Muscovites had many things to learn from the Ukrainians. To begin with, Russia received Greek Christianity by way of the Ukraine, and her church music was likewise adopted from the Ukrainians.[24] When a Ukrainian, Bortniansky, was organizing the royal choir, he got his singers from the Ukraine.[25] Ukrainian scholars were called upon by Peter the Great to aid him "westernize" Russia. He requested Archbishop Stephan Yavorsky to bring Ukrainian teachers and establish schools in the monasteries. In 1709 one of the most noted Ukrainian savants, Prokopovich, opened a school at St. Alex Nevsky, Russia.[26] But there was danger in this admiration, and, to obviate it, Russia made serious efforts to divest this culture of its Ukrainian nationality, prohibiting the usage of the name Ukraine and inventing another in its place—"Little Russia."

PARTITIONS OF POLAND AND WESTERN UKRAINE

The Poland of the eighteenth century, like that of today, was to a large extent not Polish. Besides the Poles, there were millions of oppressed Ukrainians, Lithuanians, and White Russians. Moreover, Poland had a powerless elective king, and an all-powerful parliament (sejm) in the hands of the nobles. The nobles ruled the country in their own selfish interest with a rod of iron. There were frequent turmoil and strife. Finally, Russia, Prussia, and Austria put an end to Polish anarchy by partitioning the country in three instalments, in 1772, 1793, and 1795.[27]

As independent Poland passed out of existence, her Ukrainian provinces also passed into the hands of Russia and Austria. East Galicia, Bukovina, and Ruthenia fell to Austria, the rest of the country to Russia. For better or worse the Ukrainian patriots, Bezborodko, a diplomat in the service of Russia (1793), and Rozumovsky, who was related to the Romanovs, were very anxious to unite the Ukrainian lands under Russia,[28] hoping for autonomy for their country.

Russia, however, had other intentions. After uniting a majority of the Ukrainian provinces, she began a persecution of everything that was Ukrainian. Her purpose was extermination. The public use of the Ukrainian language was prohibited. From 1876 to 1905 and from 1906 to 1917, Russia prohibited the printing of Ukrainian books[29] and the importation of books printed in other countries.[30]

The Ukrainians that were taken by Austria fared much better than their brethren under Russian rule. After many decades of struggle they won the rights of having their own schools (public and high schools), libraries, and museums, and were allowed to print newspapers, magazines, and books,[31] subject, of course, to the ever-present government censorship. Although it was the policy of Austria to grant privileges to the nationalities within her empire for the purpose of obtaining their loyalty, it was also her unfair practice to play one nationality against another. Thus the Ukrainians paid for their advantages by being subjected to Polish and Hungarian officials. Still, the oppression suffered was nothing compared to that endured in Russia, and the Ukrainians were not unmindful of the fact. They encouraged their fellow-countrymen under the czar to send their manuscripts to Galicia and had them published at Lwów.

THE UKRAINIAN RENAISSANCE

The roots of modern Ukrainian nationalism and learning go back to the Cossack period of the sixteenth to the eighteenth centuries. In the nineteenth century the Ukraine experienced a literary revival. In 1798 Ivan Kotlyarevsky, a Ukrainian nobleman of Poltava, published his travesty on the *Aeneid* in the vernacular. It created much interest among the gentry that were considered completely Russified. Other works followed by Kotlyarevsky and several other writers. It was Taras Shevchenko (1814–61), however, who was the soul of the Ukrainian renaissance.[32] He was born a serf and had a democratic influence on Ukrainian literature. "He has become the symbol of Ukrainian nationality."[33] Owing to the Russian prohibition against the Ukrainian press, several Ukrainians wrote in Russian;[34] a few others wrote in Polish.[35] In addition to the work of individual writers, the people created and preserved many songs and ballads. Indeed, "no country is so rich in folk-songs and folk-lore as the Ukraine."[36] Most of the poems—*dumy* ("rhapsodies")—go back to the Cossacks.[37]

Through the nineteenth century the Ukrainian people, although hindered in so many ways, were making progress. They cherished hopes of political independence from Russia and Austria, though it was safer to talk of self-government. A Russian revolution in 1905 deceived the people. They hoped for greater misfortune to the czarist regime and a new freedom.[38]

The moment the World War began, the Ukraine became involved. East Galicia early became a battleground and remained so until 1920, owing to the Polish-Ukrainian war for the possession of East Galicia (1919–20). The Ukrainians found themselves forced into a fratricidal struggle, some of them being compelled to fight in Austrian armies, others in Russian. Hundreds of thousands were killed and wounded. Of some thirty thousand Ukrainian Americans in the United States Army, a large number were animated by the hope of winning freedom for the country of their fathers.[39]

RISE OF THE UKRAINIAN REPUBLIC

In 1917 the Russian Revolution put an end to the old regime. The Ukrainians at once began to organize their state, and, when Kerensky would not grant self-government, the Ukraine proclaimed its independence on November 22, 1918. In the fall of 1918 the Austrian Empire fell apart, and the submerged nationalities, the Ukrainians among them, hailed a day of freedom. They began to set their political houses in order. For a while everything looked bright and promising to the Ukrainians; then Poland invaded East Galicia and fought the Ukrainians for over a year and, with the help of France, finally succeeded in subduing the province.

PARTITION OF THE UKRAINE

The Peace Conference of Paris gave East Galicia to Poland for twenty-five years; at the end of that period there was to be a plebiscite. Meanwhile, the Ukrainians were to have autonomy. In 1923, however, the Council of Ambassadors granted this Ukrainian territory to Poland without the vote or consent of the Ukrainian people. Poland also seized the Ukrainian provinces of Volhynia, Polisia, Pidliasha, and Cholm.

The Russians agreed on one thing, regardless of their other political differences—that they must keep the Ukraine. Different Russian bands of Bolsheviki, as well as the monarchists Yudenich, Denikin, and others, fought the Ukraine for nearly two years (1918–20) until they put an end to its independence.

Thus the Ukrainians gained nothing but lost enormously as a result of a world's struggle for democracy. Their country has been divided between Russia, Poland, Rumania, and Czecho-Slovakia. Although each one of the present masters of the partitioned Ukraine is bound by international treaties to guarantee self-government to the Ukrainian people, not one of these nations has lived up to its obligations. The Czecho-Slovak government was the least oppressive in Ruthenia until 1935; then, probably because of the military alliance the Czechs made with the Soviet rulers, persecution started in earnest. The climax of the Bohemian oppression of Ukrainian culture was a proclamation of the Czecho-Slovak supreme court in 1936 that the people of Ruthenia (also known as Podkarpatska Rus) cannot call themselves Ukrainians. This was in the face of the fact that there was no law in that country prohibiting one's calling one's self a Ukrainian.[40] It is unfortunate that the Bolsheviks, Poles, Rumanians, and Czechs, who themselves suffered much from foreign despotism in the past, upon gaining political ascendancy have become more inhuman than their predecessors. Religious and educational institutions are subject to constant persecution by government agents; political, social, and economic life is retarded by governmental restrictions.[41] Oppression lies heavily upon these long-afflicted people, the Ukrainians. Yet a fervent spirit remains among them. Though often brought to the point of starvation by the Bolsheviki, they keep struggling and hoping for a better future. Poland has instituted medieval terroristic practices in the Ukrainian provinces but has failed to gain her aims.[42] Once the Ukrainians learned that there was no more chance to emigrate to America, they decided to remain in their native land and hope to outlast their oppressors and become a free people.[43]

NOTES FOR CHAPTER I

1. In ancient time the official name of the country was Rus. It remained in usage until the seventeenth century. The name "Ukraina" was first recorded in 1187, then again the old chronicler used it in 1189, 1213, 1268, and 1289. The name was applied to the provinces of the kingdom of Kiev (S. Sheluchin, *The Name of Ukraine* [Vienna, 1921], pp. 13 ff.; *Ukraina* [Praha, 1936], pp. 4 ff).

2. *Ukrainian Review* (New York), March, 1931, p. 19.

3. *Encyclopaedia Americana*, XXVII (1932), 259. In 1928–29 the Ukraine produced 80 per cent of the coal, 60 per cent of the iron, and 95 per cent of the manganese of the U.S.S.R.

4. The Ukrainian people in the past also have been known under the names Ruthenian or "Rusniak" and "Little Russians" as well as under several local names, such as Lemko, Boyko, and Hutzul. The United States immigration records use the name Ruthenian and "Russniaks" in parentheses (*Senate Documents* [61st Cong., 3d sess. (Washington, 1911)], "Dictionary of Races or People," IX, 116).

5. S. Rudnitzky, *The Ukraine and Ukrainians* (Jersey City, 1915), p. 5.

6. M. Wozniak, *The Statehood of Ukraine* (Vienna, 1918), p. 9.

7. M. Hrushevsky, *History of the Ukraine* (Winnipeg, 1918), pp. 76 ff.

8. M. Arkas, *History of the Ukraine* (3d ed., Leipzig, n.d.), pp. 163–78.

9. *Ibid.*, p. 86. Anna, the daughter of King Yaroslav, married Henry I of France; another daughter, Elizabeth, married Harold, the Norwegian ruler. Yaroslav himself had a Swedish wife (C. H. Young, *The Canadian Ukrainians* [Toronto, 1931], p. 14). Monomakh, the ruler of Kiev (1113–25), married Gytha, daughter of Henry II of England.

10. "The thirteenth-century West with its painters and poets and cathedral-builders might have been wiped out by the armed hordes of Jenghis Khan had not the Ukraine met and absorbed the shock of onset" (Watson Kirk Connell, *The European Heritage* [London and Toronto, 1930], p. 9).

11. Until the recent time, in many parts of the Ukraine, mothers used to frighten their ill-behaved children thus: "The Tartars are coming, they will take you." For the Tartars carried away thousands of children and young people and sold them into slavery.

12. *Russian Empire* (London, 1856), II, 6.

13. To protect their corn from the enemy the Cossacks buried it in the ground (James Macauley, *The Natural, Statistical and Civil History of the State of New York* [Albany, 1829], II, 207).

* The works indicated by an asterisk are in Ukrainian.

14. The name "Cossack," as used by the Ukrainians, meant "free warrior," "free man."

15. W. P. Cresson, in his book *The Cossacks* (New York, 1919), has chapters on the organization and the struggle for preservation of the Ukrainian republic (chaps. iv and v).

16. About 30,000 Cossacks participated in the Thirty Years War on the side of the Protestants (B. Kusiw, "Protestantism in the Ukraine," *American Society of Church History*, VII [1928], 183).

17. The most complete study of the Cossack period is by Professor Michaila Hrushevsky in his *History of the Ukraine* (Lwów, 1922), Vol. VIII, Part II, "The Cossachina."

18. *Ibid.*, pp. 1–288 and Part III, on Khmelnitzky's period.

19. Again in 1672 Ahmed Kimprili supported the Ukrainians in war against Poland (Lord George Eversley, *The Turkish Empire from 1288 to 1914* [London, 1924], p. 174).

20. Arkas, *op. cit.*, pp. 340–49; A. A. Stonberg, *A History of Sweden* (New York, 1931), pp. 499–505.

21. Poland, even prior to 1667, ruled Western Ukraine, i.e., Galicia, Volhynia, Podolia, Pidlashe, and Cholm.

22. Wozniak, *op. cit.*, p. 29. Turkey was able to protect the southern part of the country only, as she had her wars in Central Europe at this time, trying to conquer Austria.

23. Harold H. Fisher, *America and the New Poland* (New York, 1928), p. 9.

24. G. Vernardsky, *A History of Russia* (New Haven, 1929), p. 125; also William Tooke, *View of the Russian Empire during the Reign of Catharine the Second* (London, 1800), II, 59.

25. Vernardsky, *op. cit.*; D. S. Mirsky, *Russia* (London, 1931), p. 227.

26. Baron de Monstein, *Memoirs of Russia* (London, 1770), p. 393.

27. Robert H. Lord, *The Second Partition of Poland* (Cambridge: Cambridge University Press, 1915). This book is one of the best on the subject.

28. *Ibid.*, p. 278 *et passim*. Bezborodko aimed at the re-establishment of the self-government in the Ukraine, but his aims failed to materialize.

29. In 1863 Count Voluyev, the minister of interior, decreed: "There never has existed, does not exist and there never can exist a Little Russian language and nationality" (Ralph Butler, *The New Eastern Europe* [London, 1919], p. 132).

30. A very singular incident occurred during the Russo-Japanese War. A British Bible society offered as a gift the Bible in Ukrainian to Russian soldiers. The Russian government refused the gift, but the Japanese authorities accepted the Bible for the Ukrainian prisoners. The Ukrainians who were fighting for Russia did not have the right of Japanese war prisoners (Bedwin Sands, "The Ukrainians and the War," *Contemporary Review*, CIX [March, 1916], 372).

31. Because Austria was more civilized and allowed the Ukrainians to enjoy the same rights as the other nationalities within her empire, the Russian chauvinists said that the Germans created the Ukrainians.

32. Besides Shevchenko, there were Franko, Kulish, Kotzubinsky, Fedkovich, and many others.

33. *Encyclopaedia Britannica* (14th ed.), XXII, 671.

34. To this group belong the composers Bortniansky and Chaikovsky (also

spelled in English Tschaikowsky), and the literary men Chekhov, Dostoyevsky, Gogol, Nekrasov, Kostomarov, Kovalevsky, and Korolenko (Sands, *op. cit.*, p. 376).

35. Several noted Polish authors selected their themes from the Ukraine. The "Ukrainian school" of Polish literature includes the great trio of poets, Malczewski, Zaleski, and Goszczywski (A. Bruce Boswell, *Poland and Poles* [New York, 1919], pp. 216–17).

36. Nevin O. Winter, *New Poland* (Boston, 1923), p. 256.

37. There is a critical appraisal of Maximovich's collection of 3,000 songs of the Ukraine in the *American Eclestic*, I (March, 1841), 332–51.

38. Some of the most outstanding revolutionary leaders of modern Russia were the Ukrainians Vera Zazulich, Nadia Kibalchich, Stepniak, Stefanovich, and Rodzanko (*Almanac of the Ukrainian Workingmen's Association* [Scranton, 1925], p. 5).

39. *Literary Digest*, LXIII, (November 15, 1919), 40.

40. The Ukrainian press in Europe and America proclaimed this act of Czecho-Slovakia as the darkest spot in the history of that country.

41. Rev. Basil Kusiw, "Report of the Ukrainian Evangelical Church at the Prague Conference, September 25, 1936" (mimeograph). This report refers to religious restrictions in Poland only.

42. For references on this subject see: *Manchester Guardian*, 1922–31; *Svoboda* (Ukrainian daily in Jersey City), 1918–19 and 1930–31; Herbert A. Gibbons, *Europe since 1918* (New York, 1926); E. Revyuk, *Polish Atrocities in the Ukraine* (New York, 1931); and *Current History*, February, 1931.

43. "For six hundred years, with one brief interval as an autonomous state linked with the Russian Empire, they have fought to remain Ukrainian. They have preserved their own distinctive language, their own Church, their own clothes, their high standard of husbandry. And, at the end of that fight of centuries, as at the beginning, they face the world undaunted alike by poverty, persecution, and repression—demanding the right of forty-three millions of people having a common stock and a common life to rule themselves. That demand may be resisted for a year, a generation, or a hundred generations. But at the end of that time the Ukrainian peoples will still be asking for their freedom. And there will be neither lasting peace nor the reign of justice in Eastern Europe until that right is granted, and the alien troops withdraw, leaving the Ukraine to control its own destinies and enrich all the peasant lands by its example" (H. Hessell Tiltman, *Peasant Europe* [London, 1934], p. 207).

CHAPTER II

THE EXODUS FROM THE UKRAINE

PERIODS OF EMIGRATION

THE emigration from the Ukraine to the United States seems to fall into three periods. The first was from about 1870 to 1899. It represents the beginning of mass migration and great development. During that period the United States immigration records were kept of only the countries from which the immigrants came and not of their races or nationalities. Therefore, the Ukrainians, Jews, Poles, and others were listed in American records as Russians or Austrians, according to whichever country issued their passports. Thus no one will ever know how many Ukrainians came to America during that period. The second period begins after 1899 and extends to the end of the fiscal year June 30, 1914. It was during this time that Ukrainian immigration increased by many thousands every year until it reached its highest mark in 1914—namely, 36,727 immigrants and 5,686 nonimmigrants, a total of 42,413.[1] The third period comes after 1914. The years following 1914 witnessed a decline in this movement, especially during the World War. In the early twenties this immigration was revived for a short time, but the strict new American immigration laws and the application of such laws to the Ukrainians almost completely put an end to their coming to the United States. Because the immigrants were not recorded by the American immigration officials according to their nationalities before 1899, and because the Ukraine is not an independent nation, the Ukrainians do not have their own quota under the quota law of 1924, which allows yearly admittance of only 2 per cent of the total number of a nationality present in the United States in 1890. During the years 1931–36 a total of only 587 Ukrainian immigrants were admitted, an average of 96 per year.[2]

The first occasion on which individuals among the Ukrainian

masses heard of the United States was probably about the time of the American Civil War. The Russian fleet that visited New York during the winter of 1862–63[3] no doubt had among its crew many of Ukrainian nationality. These sailors brought home news; a few also probably sent letters home in which they described America. The people in Western Ukraine most likely first heard of America from their neighbors—Czechs, Germans, and Jews.

CAUSES OF EMIGRATION

The rumors about America sounded unreal—too good to be true. The Ukrainians were the most impressed by the reports of high wages and steady employment. At home in the summertime they had to work a whole day of fourteen hours for twenty-five to thirty-five cents, while they heard that in America a laborer earned as much per hour.[4] At the same time the American dollar had a high exchange value; in Europe it produced five Austrian crowns or two Russian rubles. Such news excited them. They also learned that in the United States it was possible to acquire free homestead land. Since peasants in the Ukraine have been everlastingly land-hungry and never have enough of it, this information about American homesteads impressed them. Then, too, news spread throughout the Ukrainian villages about American freedom—religious toleration, educational opportunity, social equality, noncompulsory military service, and opportunity to improve one's self. America was a daily topic for discussion among individuals and groups. If all the stories were true, surely America was the country to seek—a "land of promise" for weary and oppressed people.

BACKGROUND OF UKRAINIAN IMMIGRANTS

The causes and incentives for emigration were numerous, but local living conditions under foreign regime constituted the chief reason for departure from the native land. The land problem itself was of primary importance. During the nineteenth century economic conditions were very bad. As there were no industries, the peasants had to remain on their farms. Rapid increase in population led to land division among the grown-up children and to subdivision in the next generation, for a peasant had no money to give his children a technical education. As a matter of fact, only a few vocational schools existed, and those located widely apart, from which the farmer's children were mostly excluded. Commerce remained mostly in the hands of the Jews, and it was next to impossible for a Gentile to succeed in the face of Jewish competition. In some parts of the country people became dreadfully impoverished. In East Galicia—the chief source of emigration, according to Ardan—the average farms (in 1870) were four acres in size.[5] Emily Balch records:

Of all the agricultural properties in the country, nearly 90 per cent are "small" (that is under twelve and a half acres), and nearly half consist of less than five acres. That this excessive subdivision is the main cause of emigration from Galicia is undisputed. When a man has so little land that it can no longer support him, much less provide for his children, he probably gets into debt, and at any rate is in imperative need of money.[6]

The small farm of a peasant was so divided that it frequently was ten feet wide and miles long. Considering the fact that in some places the country was hilly, it was impossible to till such farms even if modern implements were available. The peasants adhered mostly to the more primitive ways of their forefathers. At the same time a considerable percentage of the land in each county remained idle, partially cultivated, or under forest; it was the property of Polish or Russian landed aristocrats. When Poland conquered a part of the Ukraine, the Polish privileged classes laid claim to everything they saw. Farmers were subjected to serfdom—the serfdom that even survived the Polish independence, for it was the Austrian government, in 1848, that freed the serfs.[7] The nobles, however, retained vast estates, more property than they could or cared to use; next to the nobles, the church and monasteries possessed considerable amounts of good land. The peasant could neither buy nor rent the land from the nobles, but in some cases he was able to rent part of the church lands from the village priest. Under such conditions poverty was inevitable, and ignorance and superstition accompanied it.

In addition to the land problem, there were oppressive taxes. In order to meet the demands of the state, the landlord, and the church, a peasant in many cases had to mortgage his farm.[8] The prices on farm products were very low because of restricted demand. It did not take much produce to supply the small town population. Wages were meager, and the opportunity to earn money outside the noble's estate was very limited. There were no major industries for willing workers. To meet the annual taxes and tributes, as well as payment of other bills, peasants were forced to seek employment in neighboring countries. Late in the autumn they returned home with a precious possession—a few dollars. Such seasonal migration served as a prelude to emigration to the United States. Ivan Franko, an eminent Ukrainian poet, described the movement in its true color when he wrote:

> Oh, so spread the Ukrainian misfortune
> All over Europe, and all across the ocean.[9]

Besides economic hardship, the Ukrainian masses were oppressed socially by Russian, Magyar, and Polish officials.[10] Linguistic, religious, and educational freedom were often denied to them in their own country. Just how the Poles treated Ukrainians in East Galicia, even under Austrian rule, the following not very rare remark of a Polish teacher reveals, at least in spirit: "You are a Ruthenian dog."[11] This insult was addressed to a little sister of a man who was then editing one of the largest Ukrainian papers in America. The students in high school and university were subjected to frequent abusive remarks because they adhered to their Ukrainian nationality and religion. Economic, social, political, and educational persecutions, no doubt, retarded progress. The people were very sensitive to the social discrimination imposed upon them in their own country by a foreign ruler. Educational opportunities, even for those who could afford them, were limited.[12] Religious persecution of the Protestants by the Orthodox officials and people forced thousands to emigrate from the state of Kiev to the plains of North Dakota and to Canada.

INFLUENCE OF AMERICAN LETTERS

While the masses endured hardship, a few more daring individuals emigrated to the United States. Soon afterward came letters bringing not only good tidings about the New World but also money for relatives. The earnings in America appeared to the people of Ukrainian villages almost fabulous. When the immigrants formed the habit of sending money to their folks in East Galicia in unregistered letters, the postal clerks over there sensed the situation and commenced to steal these American

A GLIMPSE OF PEASANT LIFE IN THE UKRAINE
Planning a Future in America

letters. This practice became so widespread that at no time since has the sender been assured that his letter will reach its destination unless registered. The Ukrainian immigrants frequently complained in *Dilo*, the largest Ukrainian paper in Lwów, but it did not help matters.[13] Occasionally one of the early emigrants came back and at once became a great curiosity in his community. Neighbors and relatives came to see him and ask questions. The fact that such an "American" did not stay home any length of time, but either took his wife with him or returned alone to America for good, convinced the people that most of the stories told about that distant country were true.

STEAMSHIP AGENTS

Jewish agents played an important part in sending Ukrainians to America. In the capacity of steamship agents and money-lenders they were making large sums of money and therefore were interested in seeing the people emigrate, doing their best to persuade and assist them. It was frequently necessary to bribe the officials before the passport could be obtained, but the agents had much success in handling them. There were five thousand to six thousand such agents in Galicia alone[14]—too many for that province. Some of them used any deceitful argument to victimize people and to persuade them to emigrate to some country in the Americas. A large number of the emigrants who returned from Brazil complained bitterly because of the wrongs they had suffered owing to misrepresentation by various agents. Ukrainian papers during the last decade of the nineteenth century contained frequent warnings to their readers and their friends against the steamship agents. One editor concluded his remarks, "Yet a peasant trusts the Jew, as he believes in the gospel, because Judas Iscariot uses convincing arguments."[15] The representatives of the German transatlantic lines were very successful in sending Ukrainian and Polish peasants and workingmen and women to America. As an additional inducement, in 1877 an agent of one of the Pennsylvania coal companies, whose miners were on strike, appeared in Ruthenia and Slovakia, and persuaded many people to emigrate;[16] after this, mass migration to Pennsylvania and other states followed.

There were also other impelling motives for emigration. In Austria every young man, with very few exceptions, had to serve two or three years in the army and could not marry before completion of this military service. Under Russian rule in the Ukraine a similar situation existed. Such conditions drove thousands of boys to America, where they were able to exert more influence on their destiny. There were, also, those who, for one reason or another, had been expelled from schools and hoped to complete their education in America; likewise boys who had had only a public-school education dreamed of higher learning over there. The girls, of course, followed the boys as soon as they learned something definite of American opportunities for them, and when their parents or relatives could afford to pay for the passage.

The movement grew so quickly that in the course of a few years the Ukrainians surpassed several other nationalities contributing to the immigrant stream to America. During the decade 1899–1910, 147,375 were admitted to the United States, not counting those that were frequently registered as Austrians, Russians, or Poles.[17]

ATTEMPTS OF THE AUSTRIAN GOVERNMENT TO STOP EMIGRATION

When the mass migration to America became a question of the day even in the most remote Ukrainian villages in the provinces of East Galicia, Bukovina, and Ruthenia, there also appeared hindrances that tended to check this movement. The money question was one of the biggest problems. If it were borrowed from the Jews, the farm had to be mortgaged and a high rate of interest paid. Next to the money question there was the horror of a long voyage and the many abuses connected therewith. The greatest hindrance to emigration, however, was the opposition of the nobles and the governments of Austria and Russia: The landlords feared the loss of farm labor and the inevitable prospect of having to pay higher wages. The governments needed healthy men for the army and future wars.[18] Clergymen received orders from the Austrian government (March, 1877) to preach in the churches against emigration; they were even given a proclamation to read to intimidate people. One statement gave a warning that there was much suffering in America and that "the people would die of hunger."[19] Finally the government attempted to use force to crush emigration. It stationed guards to watch the railroad towns along the German border, but the steamship agents, representatives of the Hamburg-American and the

English Cunard lines, bribed officials and got emigrants. There were much scandal and brutality connected with the emigration traffic, such as was surpassed only by the slave trade.[20] Finally most of the restrictions on emigration were removed in the decade preceding the World War.

In the face of all the hindrances and dangers, thousands of Ukrainian peasants departed annually for the United States, Canada, and Brazil. Those that were captured by the Austrian border police and returned home would try again and again until they succeeded. The exodus involved the youth of the land, adventurers, and "those who had faith in themselves and wished to improve their position."[21]

EARLY IMMIGRANTS

Thus far it has been impossible to find out what Ukrainian was the first to emigrate to America. The first definite traces of the pioneers of this race are found during the American Civil War. It is possible, on the other hand, that some adventurous Cossacks of the Ukraine came to America even before the Revolutionary War, for it was during the reign of Empress Katherine II that the Seech fortress, the seat of the Ukrainian Cossacks, was destroyed and the self-government of the people suspended. In consequence of this many thousands of Ukrainians, especially soldiers, emigrated to foreign countries. Numerous purely Ukrainian names are found in colonial records. It is probable that the Sadovsky family of Virginia and Kentucky that played a prominent part in American public life was of Ukrainian origin. The records of the two states have the name spelled in several ways; the most frequently occurring are Sadowsky, Sandusky, and Sadowski. James was the most prominent and adventurous member of a large family. He helped George Rogers Clark to conquer the Northwest and was one of the first explorers in Kentucky.[22] The second census of the United States (1800) mentioned (p. 123) Russians in Hartford, Connecticut; it is possible that they really were Ukrainians or Jews.

If one judges by the present facts that no single Russian group, organization, or church can be found in the United States that

REV. AGAPIUS HONCHARENKO, ONE OF THE FIRST
EDUCATED UKRAINIANS IN AMERICA

does not have a few or the majority of its members of Ukrainian nationality, then it was probably true that, when Russians first visited California in 1769, there were Ukrainians among them. When Russia established Port Russ, near the present San Francisco, in 1809, she placed there between one hundred and four hundred people until the fort was given up in 1839; some of these were no doubt of Ukrainian stock.[23] As a matter of fact, the Black Sea fleet consisted mostly of Ukrainians, "the Chornomortzi." After Russia gave up Port Ross, she moved most of the people to Alaska; some remained in California. The so-called "Russian" and mixed population of Alaska in 1867 contained a few Ukrainians; for them Rev. A. Honcharenko of San Francisco published the *Svoboda and Herald*, a biweekly newspaper in Russian, English, and Ukrainian.[24] When Honcharenko came to San Francisco, on October 14, 1867, he found Ukrainian political exiles from Russia already living there. He organized them into a "Decembrist club," a political organization, which was probably the first Slavic organization of this type in America. The Russian czarist spies, however, tried to destroy it and partially succeeded.[25]

The first educated Ukrainian immigrant of whom there is an available record was Rev. Agapius Honcharenko, mentioned above, a Cossack clergyman and a political exile of high ideals. He had an interesting career. In 1857 the highest Russian church authorities sent him to Athens, Greece, to assume an office; he left his native Kiev on November 18, never to see it again. Once in an atmosphere of freedom, he felt he could read the newspapers and books he wished and correspond with whom he desired. But Russian spies pursued him for nearly twenty years in Europe and America. On his arrival in America in 1865, he taught Greek in the Episcopal school in New York and worked for newspapers until 1867, when he moved to San Francisco, there to set up a paper of his own which he published five years for the Alaskans.

After the United States purchased Alaska from Russia, Honcharenko for a while helped the American government in its Americanization of that territory, but he disapproved of the political practices of Grant's administration and broke off relations with politicians. In 1872 he purchased a small farm, where he lived to a ripe old age. Throughout his life in America, as long as he was able, he participated in social activities. He died May 16, 1915, on his farm near Hayward, California.[26]

Among the earliest Ukrainian immigrants from Galicia were George Kashnitzky, Ivan Makohon (1873), a prospector in Colorado, and M. Zalaka (1873).[27] All three of these men seem to have been successful adventurers. In 1895 Rev. Nestor Dmytriv met a man on a Ukrainian farm near Troy, New York, who had been in America twenty-seven years. The same pastor also wrote that there were Ukrainians living in Boston before 1870.[28] Besides in Massachusetts and New York, many of the first immigrants settled in the states of California, Pennsylvania, New Jersey, Illinois, Ohio, Minnesota, Michigan, and North Dakota.[29]

NUMERICAL IMPORTANCE

Most of the chroniclers of the subject give 1870 as the starting date of Ukrainian mass migration to the United States. Rev. A. Bonchevsky, one of the students of immigration, stated that before 1880 the Ukrainian immigration was sporadic; after that date it was one continuous flow.[30] In the eighties and nineties immigration increased with such force that in 1899 it was estimated there were two hundred thousand Ukrainians in America.[31] The American Immigration Commission, however, estimated that in 1897 about five hundred thousand Ukrainian immigrants lived here.[32] There is no way of substantiating these estimated figures. Apparently they were based upon European statistics and a close observation of immigrant life in American cities and industries.

Since 1899 the United States immigration authorities have tried to keep a complete record of the races and nationalities of the newcomers. The Ukrainians were recorded under the now obsolete name "Ruthenians" (Russniaks). According to the annual reports of the commissioner-general of immigration for the years 1899–1936 (fiscal year ending June 30) a total of 268,898 Ukrainian immigrants entered the ports of the United States. This figure does not include the nonimmigrants, or those who were occasionally recorded by the immigration clerks as Russians, Poles, Slovaks, Magyars, or Croats, depending upon the nationality of the clerk himself.[33]

DESTINATION

The largest number of Ukrainian immigrants gave Pennsylvania as their destination. According to immigration records, better than a third of them went there. Indeed, if one may judge their number by the institutions they maintain there, then much more than a third of the total number went to that state, either at once or moved there from other states. The closest study reveals that in 1934 there were two hundred and twenty-three Ukrainian churches in Pennsylvania. Of this number, fifty-five were under the spiritual guidance of Russian Orthodox bishops, therefore being classified as "Russian." One hundred and forty-two belonged to the Greek Catholic dioceses of bishops Bohachevsky and Takach; twenty-three were of the Ukrainian Orthodox denomination; two were Protestant churches, and one was independent. With two exceptions, all the Ukrainian mutual aid societies have their head offices in Pennsylvania.

The statistics of emigration from America to Europe (i.e., immigrants returning home) were not always kept; therefore no definite data are available on how many Ukrainians returned home every year. Some idea may be obtained from the government records for the years 1908–10, when a total of 56,076 arrived. For the same years, 6,701 departed, or about 12 departed for every 100 admitted.[34] The same would not hold true for other years, but there is a close correlation. There was a considerable number of shiftless men that made several trips back and forth before they finally settled down. Out of 147,375 who came to America during 1899–1910, 18,492 had been in the United States previously.[35] A small percentage (about 10 per cent) returned to the Ukraine after earning a few hundred dollars and remained there. Many of the immigrants have already died in America; in some cases their children, grandchildren, and a few great-grandchildren are dead also. The largest percentage died from old age; accidents in mines and mills took large tolls, and diseases due to unsanitary working and living conditions, especially tuberculosis,[36] caused the death of a considerable number.

At the present time there are in the United States more than seven hundred thousand people of Ukrainian blood, consisting of the immigrants themselves, their children, grandchildren, and in a few cases great-grandchildren. Moreover, nearly as many Ukrainians and their descendants are living in Canada, Brazil, Argentina, and Paraguay as in the United States.

NOTES FOR CHAPTER II

1. *Annual Report of the Commissioner General of Immigration* (Washington, D.C., 1915), p. 38.

2. Reports of U.S. Department of Labor, Immigration and Naturalization Service. According to these reports 158 Ukrainian immigrants came in 1931, 90 in 1932, 70 in 1933, 98 in 1934, 99 in 1935, and 72 in 1936.

3. John H. Latane, *A History of American Foreign Policy* (New York, 1927), p. 425.

4. "Emigration Conditions in Europe," *Senate Documents* (61st Cong., 3d sess. [Washington, 1911]), XII, 270.

5. Ivan Ardan, "The Ruthenians in America," *Charities*, XIII (1904–5), 246 ff.

6. *Our Slavic Fellow Citizens* (New York, 1910), p. 138.

7. Peter Roberts, *Immigrant Races in North America* (New York, 1910), pp. 27–38.

8. Julian Batchinsky, *Ukrainian Immigrant in the United States of America* (Lwów, 1914), I, 1–4.

9. Michailo Lozinsky, "The Old Country and the Ukrainians in America," *Svoboda* (Ukrainian paper, Jersey City), May 26, 1904.

10. *Senate Documents, loc. cit.*, pp. 51–63 *et passim;* John R. Commons, *Races and Immigrants in America* (New York, 1907), p. 180; Edward A. Steiner, *The Immigrant Tide, Its Ebb and Flow* (New York, 1909), p. 207.

11. Archibald McClure, *Leadership of the New America* (New York, 1916), p. 98.

12. In some districts of Galicia 56 per cent of the villages were without schools (Ardan, *op. cit.*, p. 248).

13. Michailo Pawlyk, "Ukrainians in America," *Tovarysh* (Lwów), June 14, 1888, p. 35.

14. Philip Davis, *Immigration and Americanization* (Boston, 1920), p. 76.

15. *Svoboda* (Mount Carmel, Pa.), June 1, 1899.

16. Nestor Dmytriv, "The First Steps of the Ukrainian Emigration to the United States," *Almanac of the Providence Association* (Philadelphia, 1924), p. 161; Batchinsky, *op. cit.*, p. 88.

17. *Report of the Immigration Commission* (Washington, 1911), XL, 210.

18. *Almanac of the Ukrainian Workingmen's Association* (Scranton, 1924), p. 29.

19. Balch, *op. cit.*, p. 136.

20. Batchinsky, *op. cit.*, pp. 4–15.

21. Lev Yasinchuk, *Za Oceanom* ("Beyond the Ocean") (Lwów, 1930), p. 37.

*The works indicated by an asterisk are in Ukrainian.

22. *Register of the Kentucky State History* (Frankfort), XXVII, 562, 1594; *ibid.*, XXIX, 342; *First Census of the United States* (Hampshire County, Va.), pp. 4, 24, 26, 70.

23. Sanchez-Hunt, *Short History of California* (New York, 1929), pp. 168–75.

24. *Memoirs of Honcharenko* (Kolomea, East Galicia, 1894), p. 31.

25. *Ibid.*, p. 30; Yaroslav Chyz, *"Ahapey Honcharenko," *Almanac of the Ukrainian Workingmen's Association* (Scranton, 1935), pp. 112–22.

26. *Narodna Vola* (Scranton, Pa.), June 25–27, 1929; *Oakland* (Calif.) *Tribune*, May 30, 1913.

27. Batchinsky, *op. cit.*, pp. 86–87.

28. Dmytriv, "Something about the American Ukrainians," *Svoboda* (Jersey City), May 26, 1904.

29. The immigration from 1899 to 1936, inclusively, is given by state in Appen. A.

30. Rev. An. Bonchevsky, "The Immigration in America," *Svoboda* (Jersey City), February 16, 1899; Rev. Stephan Makar, "Ukrainian Colonies in the United States," *Svoboda* (Mount Carmel, Pa.), November 4, 1897; *Report of Immigration Commission*, IX, 118; Orest Kirilenko, *Ukrainians in America* (Vienna, 1916), p. 7.

31. Makar, *op. cit.*

32. "Dictionary of Races," *Senate Documents* (61st Cong., 3d sess. [Washington, 1911]), IX, 118.

33. Batchinsky, *op. cit.*, pp. 90–91.

34. *Immigration Commission Abstract of Reports* (Washington, D.C., 1910–11), I, 112–16.

35. *Ibid.*, pp. 97, 101, 113.

36. Machailo Halko, "Memoirs of an Emigrant," *Almanac of Ukrainian Workingmen's Association* (Scranton, 1935), pp. 63–69.

CHAPTER III

FITTING INTO THE AMERICAN
INDUSTRIAL ORDER

THE FIRST CONTACT

WHEN the Ukrainian immigrants landed on American soil, their possessions were limited. In most cases they had purchased tickets to their destination in advance. This had been made possible only through a loan from local Jewish or Ukrainian userers or from relatives in America. The actual amount of cash on hand was small, ranging between ten and a hundred dollars.[1] Though lacking in material goods, a great majority of the newcomers were in their youth, their ages running from fourteen to forty-four.[2] There were more males than females, especially in the early years of immigration.[3] Healthy, strong, and ambitious, they cherished a deep desire to make the most of American opportunities. The democratic tradition of their own country fitted them for American life.

The first thing the immigrant wanted to know upon reaching his destination was when and where he might start to work. Although it was not hard to find employment in the American industrial world, the Ukrainian immigrant, naturally, was handicapped by the lack of knowledge of the English language, and ordinarily the relatives and friends to whom he had come took him to the place where they themselves were working. Frequently the newcomer went to work within a day or two after his arrival, before he fully got over seasickness, or became adjusted to American water, food, factory odors, and city smoke.

The Ukrainian immigrants were anxious to become at least superficially Americanized. They desired to know and to obey the law.[4] They wanted to resemble the natives in appearance. Being aware of the fact that their manner of dress was not American, they wanted to buy American clothes as soon as possible in order that they might not be laughed at. In this plan

26

they failed, as a rule, for a local Jewish or Ukrainian tailor persuaded the immigrants that ready-made suits were ill-fitting and that the only ones worth having were those that were made to order. Consequently they had their suits made for them, for which they generally paid, before 1914, from fifteen to thirty dollars. Such clothing had distinctive, orthodox features—long coats almost to the wearer's knees, and the trousers very wide at the hips. This type of suit was made of good material and was strong, but it differentiated its wearer from a native-born American. Most of the Slavic immigrants "fell" for such styles. Rapid Americanization, however, was by no means easy of achievement. During the first few years in this country Ukrainians seldom came into intimate contact with Americans. In most cases they settled near the mills or in the mining villages among the immigrants of other nationalities and so met an American only occasionally in the factory and on the streets.[5]

DEFICIENCIES OF THE NEWCOMERS

Although the Ukrainian immigrants had confidence and a degree of intelligence, they were severely handicapped as they began life in America.[6] American immigration records reveal that about 50 per cent of them were illiterate at the time of their arrival.[7] This was the result of Russian and Austrian educational policies among the Ukrainians. Since no technical education was available for poor people in the old country, only a few brought to America any technical knowledge.[8] Thus the newcomers swelled the ranks of unskilled labor and sought out those centers employing it.

FINANCIAL RESPONSIBILITIES

The first responsibility faced by the immigrant was that of paying off his debt for the trip to America. This ordinarily amounted to a hundred dollars. Although he had a year in which to pay it, very frequently upon arrival he borrowed the needed sum from a friend in America and sent the money to Europe. When the money arrived in the native village it created considerable excitement, for a hundred American dollars were equivalent to five hundred Austrian crowns or two hundred Russian rubles. In Europe it took years for a peasant to earn such an amount as it was believed the sender himself had earned in a few weeks. Such incidents did much to stimulate emigration and also to cause the wages of farm laborers in Ukrainian villages to rise. Notwithstanding the fact that the emigrant paid off his debt in five or six weeks instead of a year, he had to pay a high rate of interest to his creditor on the annual basis; consequently there arose prosperous money-lending individuals in many Ukrainian villages and small towns.[9] The moment the debt was paid, the immigrant began saving his money to bring over to America the members of his actual or projected family. It was also necessary for him to subsidize parents and relatives that remained in Europe. A son or daughter who failed to write home —and by writing was meant sending money—was considered "lost" or spoiled by America.

AT WORK IN THE PENNSYLVANIA MINES

A very large percentage of the newcomers settled in the mining communities, beginning with Pennsylvania.[10] The first appearance of Ukrainians in the Pennsylvania anthracite-coal mines was in the seventies (1877) in the regions of Shenandoah, Shamokin, Mt. Carmel, Olyphant, and Scranton.[11] They were induced to come to America by an agent of coal-mining companies whose workers were then on strike.[12] The experience of the first Ukrainian group in America contains some of the basic elements of that of other pioneers on this continent. When they landed in New York, they did not understand a word of English; their colorful attire attracted much attention, and they were regarded as a curiosity.[13] Being unable to get lodgings, they had to leave the city. They walked to Philadelphia, being forced to sleep outdoors because people were afraid to give shelter to such curious strangers. By the time they reached Harrisburg their energy was exhausted, but a kind-hearted American, seeing their condition, had pity on them and gave them food. Other people, however, fearful of such strangers, urged them out of town. One farmer gave them lodging, but the following night they had to sleep under a bridge. Finally they reached Shenandoah, Pennsylvania, where a Lithuanian immigrant, a business man, Carl Rice by name (in Lithuanian "Ruchus"), took care of them. Rice was a great friend of the Ukrainian immigrants to the end of his life.[14]

This group of immigrants arrived in the mining communities during a labor strike. Not understanding the conditions, or probably because of necessity, they went to work as strike-breakers; consequently they brought upon themselves the hatred of old miners, mostly Irishmen. There were frequent assaults on the strike-breakers which ended in riots. The influx of fresh immigrants tended to keep the wages low, and this prolonged the racial and labor antagonism between the Ukrainian and Irish groups. In connection with this racial animosity not infrequently the newcomer became a victim of "accidental" injury in the mine, or even death.[15] Such were the prevailing conditions in 1884, at the time of the arrival of Rev. John Volansky, the first Ukrainian Greek Catholic missionary in the United States.[16]

THE PIONEER WORK OF REV. JOHN VOLANSKY

Through the efforts of Rev. John Volansky more friendly relations were established between the Irish and the Ukrainian miners. He explained to the former that the latter were fellow-Christians and not the enemy of organized labor. This young Ukrainian pastor, the most active that ever set foot on American soil, worked to the utmost of his ability to raise the standard of living of his fellow-countrymen. He organized numerous churches in Pennsylvania and served in ministerial capacity as far west as St. Louis and Minneapolis.[17] Besides carrying on his religious functions, with the help of his able wife he organized co-operative stores, dramatic and educational clubs, and printed the newspaper *Amerika* twice a month. However, because Volansky was married and had his wife with him, American Catholic church officials induced the head of the Ukrainian church, the Metropolitan Simbratovich, to recall him after three years of noble service in America.[18] Thus the eminent missionary returned to the Ukraine, there to live until his death in 1913; but his good work for better relations between the Irish and the Ukrainian miners continues to this day.

At first the Ukrainian miners had to do the hardest kind of

work for low wages. For some of them such conditions were of short duration, either because they learned quickly the skill of mining and were promoted or because they left the mines and moved to the cities where they found employment in factories or went into the saloon business. A few miners, after saving some money, bought small farms, but the masses stuck to their jobs in the mines, and their number was continually supplemented by fresh immigrants from the Ukraine. With the increasing wave of immigration, the Ukrainians settled in practically every mining community in Pennsylvania.[19] In 1934 there were one hundred and ninety communities in that state that had Ukrainian organizations, about three-fourths of them being mining communities. In addition to the foregoing number, there are other villages with large or small unorganized Ukrainian groups.[20] In the environs of Pittsburgh the Ukrainian population is estimated at eighty thousand.[21] A conservative estimate of Ukrainian Americans in Pennsylvania—that is, immigrants and their descendants—is about three hundred thousand.[22] A majority of the men are employed in the mines; they are good workers and union men.[23] Before the present economic crisis large numbers of them saved enough of their small earnings to buy houses and, in many cases, to send their children to schools and colleges.[24] Many of the miners are protected against sickness and accident by belonging to numerous Ukrainian mutual aid associations, which also pay death benefits.

UNDERGROUND, WORK IN OTHER STATES

Pennsylvania is not the only state where Ukrainian miners settled in large numbers. It did not take some of them long to learn of the mines and wages in other states. A considerable number of them moved to the southeastern region of Ohio, where they also worked in coal mines.[25] West Virginia employs even a larger number of Ukrainian miners than Ohio; in Wheeling and adjacent communities there are close to six thousand. Among the city workers, on the other hand, are some who left the mines and now work in the factories, or have businesses of their own.[26] Much smaller groups moved to the coal-mining states farther west, although they are not, as Mr. Orth termed them, "birds of passage."[27] They settled down, bought houses, built churches, and became voters and good citizens. The mining region of southern Illinois utilizes the services of at least five hundred miners, the largest group of which settled at Zeigler, where they have two churches.[28] Nearly two hundred settled in the coal-mining regions of Texas, especially at Thurbert and Bremond.[29]

Wyoming and North Dakota likewise have coal miners of Ukrainian extraction. In 1936 about sixty Ukrainian families lived in the mining communities of Sublet and Frontier in the former state. In North Dakota the first settlers in the place now called Wilton were the Ukrainians that came there in 1897. When the coal mines opened, over one hundred Ukrainian families and about twenty-five single men settled in the vicinity. As long as the mines used man power instead of machinery, these people remained, but during the last few years the steam shovel has displaced men at work in the open mines. The miners that were left without work either took up farming or stayed in the city to await better times. This has had serious effects upon their savings.[30]

DIVERSE MINING

Coal mining is not the only type of mining employing Ukrainian labor. The diverse mining of New Jersey and Colorado employs its share of workers of this nationality. In 1905, Denver, Colorado, had over three hundred Ukrainian families; the city of Pueblo had a similar number, although the immigration records do not disclose these facts. Owing to the high altitude, however, some families were compelled to move to other states.[31] In 1903 a much smaller group settled in the vicinity of the lead and zinc mines of Desloge and St. Francois, Missouri, but there was a sufficient number of them at the former place to establish various organizations, including a Greek (Rite) Catholic church, which was built in 1905. In the deep depression of 1932 these mines worked only three days per week, and here likewise some miners took up farming.[32]

As soon as the iron mines opened in northeastern Minnesota,

the Ukrainian immigrants followed the movement in that direction, and today the iron-mining communities of Chisholm, Hibbing, Eveleth, Virginia, and others count Ukrainian groups in the polyglot element of their population. In Chisholm they have two churches within the space of two city blocks.[33] As evidence of better days of the past, as well as of thrift, most of the miners in this region own their own homes.

Another iron-mining state that employs a few Ukrainian workers is Michigan. Ironwood probably has the largest single group on the range—about fifteen families—but there are a few scattered in Bessemer and other communities. At Ironwood there is a Ukrainian lodge or self-aid society, the chief seat of which is at Homestead, Pennsylvania.

DOMESTIC HARDSHIPS

Life in the mining villages, until the appearance of automobiles and radios, was dull. Everything, including the daily work, the appearance of company houses, and the village itself bespoke monotony. The only variety was that of the immigrant elements, and the language of the immigrant miners consisting of their native tongue plus the newly acquired words learned from miners of other nationalities, and always a few inserted English words with foreign endings.[34]

A typical feature of the mining community was the crushing burden borne by the miner's wife. During the last two decades of the nineteenth century and the first decade of the twentieth, the life of a Ukrainian miner's wife was almost always one of continuous toil and hardship. When she came to America and a mining village, she was, as a rule, young, healthy, and not infrequently good looking. After several years' residence in her adopted environment, her health was depleted, and she was, in some cases, aged beyond recognition. She cared not only for her husband and from three to ten, or even more, children but often for roomers and boarders also. From six to twelve of these crowded all the available space of the dwelling. The house was usually rented from the mining company, the rent averaging seven dollars per month, unfurnished. This was deducted from the worker's pay. The miner's wife alone had to do all the house-work—washing, cleaning, and cooking for ten to twenty people. In most cases she had to bring all the grocery supplies from the company store, from which employees were obliged to buy.[35] Twice each month the miner's wife had to contend with the anxieties incident to payday—days of drunkenness, singing, arguments, and occasional fighting. A similar situation also existed among the mill workers in larger cities. In 1914 it was almost impossible to find a lodging among the Ukrainians in Pittsburgh where absolute sobriety existed on a payday or over the week end. There were only a few families where no drunkards were kept or intoxicating liquors permitted. Pittsburgh was no exception. Such conditions prevailed until national prohibition went into effect; then matters improved considerably, probably because liquor was harder to obtain and there was more chance of arrest with disgrace attached thereto. Consequently the prohibition law was a blessing to the Ukrainian immigrants as a class. Few singular exceptions of law violation existed among them during this period.

URBAN OCCUPATIONS

The largest centers of Ukrainian population in the United States are the industrial cities: Boston, Hartford, New York, Buffalo, Rochester, Newark, Philadelphia, and Pittsburgh in the East; Chicago, Milwaukee, Detroit, St. Louis, and Minneapolis in the Middle West; and San Francisco and Los Angeles on the Pacific coast.[36] It is, undoubtedly, because of the numerous opportunities city life offers that many prefer it to that in the mining communities.[37]

Upon their arrival in America very few Ukrainian immigrants, as already noted, were skilled workers. Each of them, therefore, tried to get any work that he could find and was able to do until he could obtain something better. As most were of the laboring class, they commonly found employment in the following industries: iron and steel, glass, rubber, textiles, shoes, furniture, automobiles, cameras, and, in later years, radios. The iron and steel manufacturing districts of Pittsburgh, Youngstown, and

Gary employ thousands of Ukrainian workers in various departments. They often join labor unions while working in industrial plants. In 1887 one factory in Pittsburgh discharged sixty Ukrainian workers because they belonged to a labor-union organization.[38] The flour mills of Minneapolis find their labor useful; the meat-packing houses of Chicago and Omaha likewise. Probably no other single industry employs as many Ukrainian workers as does automobile manufacture in different cities of Michigan and wherever other branch factories are located. There are also many Ukrainians working in various smaller industries, such as the manufacture of carpets, electrical supplies, rope, the refining of sugar, and the preparation of fish products; these are more local in character.[39] Railroads at first attracted only an insignificant number of these people. This was because of the fact that in most cases knowledge of English was necessary, and before an immigrant acquired it, unless he worked among his own countrymen, he was subject to ridicule. In recent years more Ukrainians have entered railroad industries to be employed as laborers, clerks, and depot agents.

According to the case studies made by the immigration authorities during the years 1909-10, a very large number of Ukrainians engaged both in specialized and diversified industries.[40] Their weekly earnings at that time were $9.92-$13.89; a few earned more, a few less.[41] During the World War, wages went up, as did the standard of living. However, in 1922, industries in Pittsburgh, Pennsylvania, paid as low as thirty and thirty-two cents per hour to unskilled laborers, while mechanics were paid forty-eight and one-half cents, fifty cents, and sixty cents per hour.[42]

Some Ukrainians in America work as carpenters, plumbers, printers, mail carriers, bricklayers, tailors, bakers, barbers, photographers, shoemakers, drivers, and garage mechanics.[43] A few, both immigrants and their descendants, are engaged in janitorial work in public-school and business buildings. A small group entered business, manufacturing, and the professions.[44] In more recent years a considerable number of professional athletes have appeared before the public in baseball, football, wrestling, and pugilism.[45] Hundreds of Ukrainians invaded the lumber camps of Washington and Wisconsin. Individuals are scattered all over the country in all kinds of useful work.[46] Indeed, it may be said that the "old stock" of Ukrainian Americans can work by the side of laborers of every nationality and get along well, except with the Poles and Mexicans.[47]

WOMEN IN INDUSTRY

The city occupation of Ukrainian women deserves consideration because frequently women work in the same factory with the men, only at easier jobs, for shorter hours (thanks to the laws of various states), and for smaller wages.[48] At one time they were an important factor in the textile as well as the iron and steel industries. Owing to the fact that many more men than women came to America from the Ukraine, most of the girls were soon married. Marriage, on the other hand, did not always prevent them from working in various industrial establishments, although Ukrainian girls prefer housework to factory employment.[49] Because of this preference, one of their countrymen established an employment office in New York City which specializes in placing girls in domestic service.[50] In large cities hundreds of poor Ukrainian immigrant women work at night cleaning offices in numerous establishments. In New York City they have their units of labor union. A considerable number of girls in recent years have found employment in the restaurants, hotels, and department stores.[51] Those possessing professional skill, such as stenography, nursing, designing, and teaching, are found in every large city in the East.[52] About twenty are under civil service in Washington, D.C. A few enterprising women have businesses of their own, mostly beauty parlors, dressmaking establishments, restaurants, and small stores.[53]

INDUSTRIAL PROGRESS AND ECONOMIC AND SOCIAL IMPROVEMENT

American life has proved to be a great education for many of the expatriate Ukrainians. As before stated, at the time of their arrival in America a majority did not know any trade and, as a result, had to do the hardest manual labor for low wages. After a few years of residence in America, some individuals were advanced to the position of foreman in their respective places of employment; others that had the ambition to study acquired useful mechanical knowledge, a trade, or profession. People who were easily satisfied with what they had made no progress.[54] On the whole, the immigrants and their children were such adept pupils that today one finds them in nearly every trade in America.[55] But many of them even now are at a disadvantage because they speak English with a Ukrainian accent; nevertheless, they are able to hold their places in the world of competition.

With improvement in skill has come economic and social betterment. Only a very few, probably a fraction of 1 per cent, however, have attained the status of "rich," as defined by their countrymen. Although many of them were victims of professional swindlers and bank failures in the past,[56] and others had their savings depleted by appeals for money from relatives and institutions abroad, a large percentage by thrifty living have tasted a measure of prosperity. Especially during and immediately after the war a considerable number of them invested in homes.[57] Although their homes often approach the American standard, even now a majority of them still live in the poorer sections of American cities. Besides building homes they erected impressive-looking church buildings and of late years have taken to constructing community centers, the so-called "Ukrainian homes," which as civic centers house their citizens' clubs as well as other political and social organizations, and also occasionally a Ukrainian school (for the study of the Ukrainian language).

It is to be noted that another type of social improvement has accompanied economic betterment. In the larger congregations, where formerly half of the people were illiterate and the other half merely able to read and write, one finds today not only more literacy among the adults but also high-school and even university graduates, especially among the second and third generations. As among all immigrant groups, there are parents whose attitude toward the education of their children is negative, and there are those who, although themselves uneducated, are anxious for the educational welfare of their family.[58] The children

UKRAINIAN NATIONAL HOME IN CHESTER, PENNSYLVANIA

of business men are fortunate, for the most part, in that they almost always can secure a higher education if they themselves wish one. In most cases the parents, particularly the mother, have acquired some knowledge of English, if not from other sources, then from their children. The latter not infrequently have tutored their parents in preparation for the taking out of citizenship papers. A majority of the men immigrants and probably a third of the women are American citizens.

THE EFFECTS OF THE ECONOMIC DEPRESSION

The recent economic depression was a severe setback to nearly all the Ukrainian Americans. During those years only a few, as a rule, in each community were able to work steadily. Those that were engaged in business fared much better, although some of them had to discontinue. A very large percentage of these people had their life-earnings "frozen" or completely lost in the banks. With no work and no funds, they endured great hardships until the governmental agencies came to their rescue.

Communities where no one was on relief have been rare. Where no municipal, county, or federal relief was available, a few people in various parishes received aid from their church relief committees or from Ukrainian mutual aid societies. In some cities where it was absolutely impossible for men to get jobs, their wives and daughters volunteered to go out to work to help maintain the family. There were families who endured much suffering but who would not go on relief; then again there were others, often persuaded by the bolsheviki, who applied for relief too readily. During the darkest years of the depression, a very large number of the population, especially in the mining regions of Pennsylvania, had to seek assistance. But even then the small aid received did not obviate suffering, particularly that of widows with children.[59]

In consequence of unemployment a considerable number of Ukrainians lost their homes. While they have been able to maintain their churches, though heavily mortgaged, they lost a score or more of their newly built "national homes." However, by 1935 and 1936, a sufficient number of people in several of the large cities had employment again so that a drive could be started to regain some of the public buildings lost or to erect new halls.

NOTES FOR CHAPTER III

1. The amount of money shown by the group of 1904 was $10.51 per capita (Prescott F. Hall, *Immigration* [New York, 1906], p. 71).

In the fiscal year ending June 30, 1910, there came to the United States 27,907 Ukrainian (Ruthenian) immigrants. They possessed the following sums of money on arrival: $50 or over, 439; less than $50, 25,412. Total amount shown, $569,776 (*Annual Report of the Commissioner General of Immigration for the Fiscal Year Ended June 30, 1910*, p. 21).

2. Of the 36,727 that came in the fiscal year ended June 30, 1914, there were 2,680 under fourteen years of age; 32,579 in the ages fourteen to forty-four years; and 1,468 were forty-five years and over (*ibid.*, *1915*, p. 42).

3. According to the immigration records, 147,375 Ukrainians came to America during the decade from 1899 to 1910. Of this number, 74.4 per cent were males and 25.6 per cent females ("Distribution of Immigrants," *Senate Documents* [61st Cong., 3d sess.], XX, 47 ff.).

4. The best proof for this statement may be found in any city with a large Ukrainian population. According to a letter from the *Scranton Times* to the author (December 1, 1931), the Ukrainians in that city are "good citizens." As a further evidence of good citizenship, the police record in Scranton for 1931 reveals that there were only two arrests of the Ukrainians out of the estimated 12,000–15,000.

In the city of Wheeling and vicinity, with the Ukrainian population more than 1,000, not a single arrest was made, and no case came up in court, during the thirty months of the pastorate of Rev. H. Kovalsky (*letter from Rev. Humphrey Kovalsky to the author, March 2, 1932).

Shamokin, Pennsylvania, a town with a large Ukrainian population, has not had a single arrest or case in court during the last twelve years. Both the old and the young generations are good citizens (*letter from A. C. Drozdiak to the author, January 4, 1933).

5. Rev. A. Bonchevsky, in the *Svoboda* (Jersey City), February 16, 1899.

6. "No more intelligent peasants exist than those of Ruthenia" (Minnie Murier Davie, "In Ruthenia," *Living Age*, November 1, 1890, p. 371); "The Ukrainians work hard, fight hard, and play hard. They are blessed with an elastic temperament" (Nevin O. Winter, "The Ukraine, Past and Present," *National Geographic Magazine*, August, 1918, p. 458).

7. Jeremiah W. Jenks and W. J. Lauck, *The Immigration Problem* (New York, 1913), p. 142; V. Biberovich in the *Svoboda* (Jersey City), August 24, 1933.

* The works indicated by an asterisk are in Ukrainian.

8. The United States Immigration records for 1899–1910 present the following facts about the occupation of the Ukrainian immigrants before coming to America:

PROFESSIONAL

Actors	3	Musicians	11
Architects	1	Physicians	3
Clergy	47	Sculptors and artists	6
Editors	1	Teachers	24
Electricians	1	Other professions	4
Engineers	1		
Lawyers	2	Total professional	109
Literary and scientific persons	3		

SKILLED

Bakers	34	Milliners	3
Barbers and hairdressers	3	Miners	189
Blacksmiths	278	Painters and glaziers	26
Bookbinders	1	Photographers	3
Brewers	4	Plasterers	3
Butchers	60	Printers	11
Cabinet-makers	13	Saddlers and harness-makers	8
Carpenters and joiners	442	Seamstresses	42
Clerks and accountants	64	Shoemakers	366
Dressmakers	58	Stokers	9
Engineers (locomotive, marine)	6	Stonecutters	10
Engravers	1	Tailors	376
Furriers and fur-workers	20	Tanners	25
Gardeners	11	Textile-workers	7
Hat- and cap-makers	2	Tinners	11
Iron- and steel-workers	36	Tobacco-workers	2
Jewelers	2	Watch- and clockmakers	2
Locksmiths	114	Weavers and spinners	48
Machinists	14	Wheelwrights	59
Mariners	17	Woodworkers	14
Masons	114	Other skilled	37
Mechanics (not specified)	10		
Metal-workers	9	Total skilled	2,595
Millers	31		

MISCELLANEOUS

Agents	1	Laborers	47,746
Bankers	1	Merchants and dealers	44
Draymen and teamsters	4	Servants	21,690
Farm laborers	55,693	Other miscellaneous	40
Farmers	535		
Hotel-keepers	2	Total miscellaneous	125,756

No occupation (including women and children) 18,915

Grand total 147,375

("Distribution of Immigrants," *Senate Documents* [61st Cong., 3d sess.], XX, 153–55).

9. They included Jews and rich Ukrainian peasants.

10. From 1899 until June 30, 1933, the United States received 268,311 Ukrainian immigrants; 114,179 gave Pennsylvania as their destination (see Appen. A, pp. 150-53).

11. Julian Batchinsky, *Ukrainian Immigration in the United States of America*, (Lwów, 1914), I, 88-135.

12. Among the first Ukrainian miners were the following: John Mucha, Joseph Zohak, S. Murza, John Glova, and Anthony Luchkovich. This group came from the same place—Ustia Ruske, East Galicia (Stephen Makar in the *Svoboda* [Mount Carmel, Pa.], November 4, 1897).

13. Volodimir Korolenko's novel *Without a Language* (Lwów, 1918) gives an idea of some of the hardships suffered by early Ukrainians in America because they had no knowledge of the English language.

14. People traded with him, went to him with all their problems, and solicited his advice. His business was so multifarious that it served most of the needs of immigrant miners (Dr. Volodimir Simenovich, "Ukrainian Immigration in the United States," *Ukraina* [Ukrainian weekly paper; Chicago], March 13, 1931).

15. A few remaining old miners and their children frequently tell of the days of early hardship.

16. A program of the tenth anniversary of Rev. Michael Guriansky's pastorate of the St. Cyril and Methodius Ukrainian Greek Catholic Church of Olyphant, Pennsylvania, October 28, 1930; Simenovich, *op. cit.*

17. Batchinsky, *op. cit.*, p. 257.

18. The Ukrainian Greek Catholic (Uniate) clergy are allowed to marry, although they recognize the pope at Rome as the church head.

19. Almost 52 per cent at the time of their arrival designated Pennsylvania as their goal (Emily Balch, "*Our Slavic Fellow Citizens* [New York, 1910], p. 267; Archibald McClure, *Leadership of the New America* [New York, 1916], p. 97).

20. For the communities with Ukrainian population see Appen. B; cf. also Wasyl Halich, "Ukrainians in Western Pennsylvania," *Western Pennsylvania Historical Magazine* (Pittsburgh) June, 1935, pp. 139-46.

21. "Ukrainians in America," *Literary Digest*, LXIII (November 15, 1919), 40.

22. See Appen. B.

23. The official of the United Miners stated the fact that the Ukrainians are more interested in the union than are the English-speaking people and pay their fees more promptly (*Svoboda* [Scranton], June 29, 1905). Of the 166 cases in the anthracite-coal mining studied by the Immigration Commission, 128 (77.1 per cent) were affiliated with the trade unions ("Immigrants in Industries," *Senate Documents* [61st Cong., 3d sess.], LXXVII, 620).

24. The average earnings of Ukrainian miners before 1910 had been $1.98 per day. The earnings increased with the years of experience (*ibid.*, LXVIII, 26, 50, 60-70).

25. There are smaller organized groups of Ukrainians in the following Ohio mining villages: Barton, Bellaire, Powhatton, Bridgeport, and Yorkville. There are many scattered in other communities.

26. In Wheeling and suburbs there were (in 1932) about 300 Ukrainian families and about 60 single men. They also lived in Clarksburg, Sabraton, Weirton, Algona, Benwood, Glendale, McKeefery, Morgantown, Scarbo, Tams, Thomas,

and Windsor Heights (letter from Rev. Humphrey Kovalsky to the author, March 2, 1932).

27. Samuel P. Orth, *Our Foreigners* (New Haven: Yale University Press, 1920), p. 169.

28. Some of those miners are still backward and call themselves "Russians" or "Rusniaks," while all of them are Ukrainians from the provinces of East Galicia and Ruthenia and speak Ukrainian (*letter from Michael H. Aleksick to the author, January 25, 1932).

29. P. Kmita, *"Ukrainians in Texas," *Svoboda* (New York), October 24, 1907.

30. In 1933 there were in Wilton and on the farms north of the city 102 families and 16 single men.

31. Investigation of Julian Batchinsky, *op. cit.*, p. 121.

32. "Ukrainians in the Lead Mines of Missouri," *Svoboda* (Jersey City), September 4, 1913; letter from Rev. Michael Lukasky to the author, March 9, 1932.

33. The town of Chisholm, Minnesota, seems to have an almost entirely foreign population, mostly Slavic—Serbian, Slovenian, and Ukrainian. The last-named occasionally call themselves "Carpatho-Russians." The Ukrainians had two Greek Catholic churches in 1932, both of which were without pastors.

34. Such practice is prevalent among most of the American immigrants regardless of racial origin.

35. According to government reports, "some of these houses that rented for $16.00 per month, or $192.00 a year, are stated to have cost the company when new $550.00 each" ("Immigrants in Industries," *Senate Documents* [61st Cong., 3d sess.], LXVIII, 545).

36. The cities having the largest estimated Ukrainian population are: New York, 50,000–75,000; Newark, 6,000; Yonkers, 5,000; Pittsburgh, 15,000; Philadelphia, 5,000; Youngstown, Ohio, 5,000; Cleveland, 10,000; Northampton, Pennsylvania, 5,000; Scranton, 12,000–15,000; Chicago, 15,000; Detroit, 10,000; and Boston, 4,000.

37. Howard B. Gross, *Aliens or Immigrants* (Cincinnati, 1906), p. 180.

38. *Tovarysh* (Lwów), June 14, 1888, p. 41.

39. The Alexander Smith Carpet Shop and the Otis Electric Company, of Yonkers, New York, employ hundreds of these people (letter from Rev. Volodimir Spolitakevich to the author, December 1, 1931).

40. A large number are employed in rope manufacturing and fish products in Brooklyn, New York (letter from Rev. Anthony Lotovich to the author, March 1, 1933).

41. "Immigrants in Manufacturing and Mining," *Senate Documents* (61st Cong., 3d sess.), VII, 337–39, 365–67, gives Cases 1–3.

42. *Narodna Vola* (Scranton), June 27, 1922.

43. Nicholas Ceglinsky, "How the Ukrainians Came," *The Interpreter* (New York City), January, 1924, p. 7.

44. Chap. v deals with this topic more fully.

45. The most noted Ukrainian pugilists are Steve Halaiko, of Auburn, N.Y., a one-time member of the United States Olympic team, and John Jadick, junior welterweight champion, whose home is in Philadelphia (*Milwaukee Journal*, January 24, 1932). The wrestlers are numerous; the more conspicuous are Nick Goch (Vanka Zelizniak, who is frequently advertised as "just from Russia"), Nazarinoff, Horkavenko, Piddubny, and the all-American football player, Nagurski. The baseball leagues have any number of Ukrainian players, but up to 1936 the only two

CASE 1

CITY OCCUPATION OF 313 UKRAINIAN MALES AND 34 FEMALE WORKERS

Occupation	Male	Female
Carpet manufacturing	4	5
Car-building and repair	224	. . . .
Cuttery- and tool-manufacturing .	1	. . . .
Electric-railway transportation . .	1	. . . .
Foundry and machine shop . . .	34	11
Hosiery and knit goods	7	3
Locomotive-building and repair . .	3	. . . .
Paper and wood-pulp manufacturing	2	. . . .
Rope, twine, and hemp manufacturing	21	15
Sewing-machine manufacturing . .	13	. . . .
Steam-railway transportation . .	1	. . . .
Zinc-smelting and manufacturing .	1	. . . .

CASE 2

PERCENTAGE OF THE UKRAINIAN IMMIGRANTS ENGAGED IN EACH
SPECIFIED INDUSTRY

(Number Reporting Complete Data 1,878 [Male, 1,048, and Female, 830]
16 Years of Age or Over)

Industry	Male	Female
In agricultural pursuit	0.0	0.1
In domestic service	0.3	1.2
In manufacturing and mechanical pursuits	64.0	32.2
In mining	29.1	0.0
In general labor	1.1	0.0
In trade	1.5	0.4
In transportation	0.6	0.0
At home	3.3	66.0
At school	0.0	0.1

(*ibid.*, Table 21, p. 365).

CASE 3

WAGES OF THE UKRAINIAN INDUSTRIAL EMPLOYEES 18 YEARS
OF AGE OR OVER

(Total Number Reporting, 385; Average Weekly Earnings, $9.92)

Under $2.50 . . . . 0.0
$2.50 and under $5.00 . . . . 0.5
$5.00 and under $7.50 . . . . 14.8
$7.50 and under $10.00 . . . . 42.1
$10.00 and under $12.50 . . . . 29.3
$12.50 and under $15.00 . . . . 5.2
$15.00 and under $17.50 . . . . 6.8
$17.50 and under $20.00 . . . . 0.8
$20.00 and under $22.50 . . . . 0.3
$25.00 or over 0.3

(*ibid.*, p. 375).

who succeeded in the majors were Guzelak and Urbanski (*Svoboda* [Jersey City], November 9, 1932).

46. This is according to the statement of Mr. Dutkanich, of Chicago, who has traveled considerably as a salesman.

47. The first few years the Molokane sect had a good deal of misunderstanding with the Mexican laborers in Los Angeles, although they were at peace with all other people (*Senate Documents*, LXXXV, Part III, 456).

48. The 46 female workers reported average weekly earnings of $6.52, which was far below the native American average of $8.04 (*ibid.*, VII, 368).

49. Ardan, *op. cit.*, p. 249.

50. It was the Thompkins Square Employment Agency (Eighth St. and Third Ave.). Its advertisement in the *Svoboda* (Jersey City), April 28, 1933, guaranteed $25–$40 per month with board and room for domestic servants.

51. In the years of depression, when men were unable to get employment, many of the Ukrainian women, wives and daughters, came to the rescue of their families because they were able to get some employment (*letter from Rev. H. Kovalsky to the author, March 2, 1932; Rev. Joseph Zelechivsky, "Short Description of the Beginnings of Ukrainian Immigration in Boston, Massachusetts" [MS], to the author, July 9, 1931).

52. The Ukrainians of Olyphant, Pennsylvania, hold the record among their countrymen in having (in 1932) 29 graduate nurses and 6 schoolteachers. In 1933 there were 84 girls of Ukrainian descent teaching school in eleven states (W. Halich, in the *Svoboda* [Jersey City], August 15, 1933).

53. *Almanac of the Ukrainian Women* (New York, 1931), p. 105.

54. A recent traveler in mining villages of Pennsylvania described the unprogressive communities as having small houses built close together. The houses are unclean and have no gas, electricity, or water. Each house has several children who are growing up in filthy streets. The church is the only place where the people meet once a week, but the priests are not doing much to elevate them to a higher level of life (*Narodna Vola* [Scranton], February 16, 1924).

55. Ceglinsky, "Ukrainians in America," *The Interpreter* (New York), December, 1924, p. 6.

56. In most of the cases, the swindlers were steamship agents, Ukrainian or others, who took the people's hard-earned money to transmit to relatives in Europe and never sent it. Such criminals took at least $200,000 from Ukrainian immigrants. A certain Ukrainian agent by the name of Choma ran away from Pittsburgh with $100,000 (Yasinchuk, *Za Oceanom* [Lwów, 1930], p. 85). In Chicago a certain Jew by the name of Kanto pretended to have an agency that sent money to Europe and embezzled larger sums until the government officials put an end to his evil activities (Edith Abbott, *Immigration: Select Documents and Case Records*, pp. 698–99). During 1916–17, in many cities of the United States and Canada, there traveled, under various assumed names, a Pole by the name of Kenska, who established "bureaus" and collected money from the Polish and Ukrainian people to send to Europe. He had such an "office" in his living room in Bloomfield, New Jersey. As he operated mostly through the mail, the United States postal officials got on his trail and finally caused his arrest in Boston.

57. It is impossible to substantiate by statistical figures what percentage of Ukrainian Americans own their homes, especially in large cities. The following accounts, however, give some idea: "Immigrants in Industries," *Senate Documents*,

LXVIII, 452 contains a statement that, next to the Germans, the Ukrainians lead all the immigrants in home ownership. No figures were given. The latest accounts on this topic from several communities give some idea in regard to present home-ownership:

Case 1: Ukrainian Presbyterian Church, Newark, N.J. Of 143 members (including young people), 31 own their homes (letter from Rev. A. Kuman to the author, February 10, 1937).

Case 2: Ukrainian Catholic Church, Baltimore, Md. About 200 families; majority own their own homes (letter from Rev. Wasyl Manovsky to the author, February 14, 1937).

Case 3: St. Peter and Paul's Ukrainian Catholic Church, Cambridge, Pa. Out of 274 families, 162 own their homes (letter from Rev. Dr. N. Kopachuk to the author, February 20, 1937).

Case 4: Ukrainian Catholic Church, Woonsocket, R.I. About two-thirds of the members own their homes (letter from Rev. Wasyl Tremba to the author, February 11, 1937).

Case 5: Freeland, Pa. Only about 25 per cent of the Ukrainian miners own their homes there (letter from Rev. B. Machnyk to the author, February 18, 1937).

The *Jubilee Book* (Jersey City, 1936) contains the following statements in regard to homeownership:

1. West Allis, Wis. Of 17 families, all own their homes (p. 747)
2. Stapleton, N.Y. Nearly all of the 65 families own their homes (p. 642)
3. Palmerton, Pa. There are about 100 Ukrainian families, the majority of whom own their homes (p. 712)
4. Woodhaven and Ozone Park, N.Y. Out of 50 families, all but 3 own their homes (p. 654)
5. In McAdoo, Pa., 69 out of about 100 families own their homes (p. 704)

58. Mr. Young gives a picture of a Ukrainian Canadian farmer, father of six, all of whom are college graduates (Charles H. Young, *The Ukrainian Canadians* [Toronto: Nelson & Sons, Ltd., 1931], p. 182).

59. Not all of the Ukrainian communities tackled the depression in the same way, but in the end a majority of them had to seek some kind of help. No Works Progress Administration (W.P.A.) office approached could furnish any data in regard to the nationality of people working on various projects. The Ukrainian accounts are only general observations. According to the *Jubilee Book*, the Ukrainians of McAdoo, Pa. (p. 704), Brooklyn, N.Y. (p. 609), and South Chicago (p. 543) knew almost no depression because almost every worker had work. At the same time the people of the Pennsylvania anthracite region suffered very much and over half of them had to seek help (letter from Rev. B. Machnyk to the author, February 18, 1937). In Baltimore, Md., a committee of the Ukrainian Catholic Church aided indigent members; about 10 per cent of the congregation needed help, some of whom accepted it unwillingly (letter from Rev. W. Manovsky, February 14, 1937). In Ambridge, Pa., Rev. O. Mycyk, then pastor of the Ukrainian Orthodox Church, while visiting his people learned of one family that had had nothing to eat for two days and refused to apply for relief. Only a small percentage sought relief there (letter from Rev. O. Mycyk to the author, February 17, 1937; letter from Rev. N. Kopachuk, February 20, 1937). From these and many other evidences it is apparent that the Ukrainians, like many other people, in the face of starvation had to apply for help.

CHAPTER IV

CONTRIBUTION TO AMERICAN AGRICULTURE[1]

THE BEGINNING OF AGRICULTURAL COMMUNITIES

ALTHOUGH agriculture was the main economic interest in the homeland, the Ukrainian immigrants did not always turn to farming on their arrival in the United States.[2] The country and its language were strange to them. Practically all were without the capital necessary to start farming, and they were afraid to purchase land on borrowed money. The result was that a considerable number who ultimately became farmers worked in industries for several years to accumulate the necessary capital. On the other hand, an equally large number emigrated with their families from the provinces of East Galicia, Bukovina, and Kiev with the definite purpose of becoming farmers in the new land. They were, for the most part, the people who took up homesteads in North Dakota, Montana, and Canada.

In the beginning, Ukrainian farming in America was an individual rather than a group undertaking, and this feature was characteristic for many years. As there was no organization to guide or direct the immigrants to farms, their agricultural communities were settled sporadically and were widely scattered.[3] There was likewise no Ukrainian government to encourage or aid the formation of agricultural colonies in America.[4] An individual, having bought a farm in a community that pleased him, informed relatives and friends, who followed him. Occasionally these pioneer farmers appealed to their countrymen through the Ukrainian press in America. They pointed to the advantages of farm life as compared with the dangerous and unsanitary conditions in the mines and mills. Their strongest points of appeal were the independence of farmers and the satisfaction of owning land. Such arguments impressed Ukrainian immigrants favorably as they were individualists by nature.

Although a few settled on farms immediately after the Civil War, the main movement to the land took place during the years after 1890.[5] It slackened for a time during the World War, apparently because of the high wages in industrial centers and because many were serving in the American army. This was particularly true of the Ukrainians of Chicago, who had been moving to farms in Indiana and Wisconsin.

MANNER OF SETTLEMENT

When the Ukrainians turned to farming, the best land was already occupied, and they had to take what was left. There were several alternatives—the purchase of developed farms with modern buildings, the acquisition of barren and cutover land, much of it unfit for settlement, or homesteading in the Dakotas, Montana, and Wyoming. Lack of capital prevented the purchase of high-priced improved farms. Yet, it is interesting to note that most of the Ukrainian farmers in America are landowners, the number of renters and hired laborers being insignificant.[6]

THE DISTRIBUTION IN NEW ENGLAND

The Ukrainian farmers in New England are widely scattered.[7] Individuals have been farming there for nearly fifty years; group settlements, however, are a more recent development. Many bought so-called "abandoned" farms, and, just as the New Englanders of early Colonial times turned to the sea or moved westward, so many of their Ukrainian and other Slavic successors who settled on the same farms two hundred and fifty years later were forced to supplement the family income from elsewhere. Many of them worked in factories of the near-by cities where there was employment and tended the farms part-time and with the help of their families. Frequently the men worked in the mills during the day and returned to their farms in the evening. Such part-time farmers are common along the coast.

One of the largest Ukrainian rural settlements of New England is at South Deerfield, Massachusetts.[8] Other groups of considerable size are located near Colchester, Orange, Oxford, and Willimantic, Connecticut; Rutland, Vermont; and Manchester,

New Hampshire. These communities have about forty Ukrainian farmers each and support their own churches and other social institutions. Like other immigrant farmers in this section, they experiment in an effort to get the most out of the soil and make it pay. In many cases they are successful and make a living from their small farms. Those situated near the cities confine their attention to gardening, poultry, dairying, and hog-raising, as they have a market near at hand. The settlements in the interior also raise grain crops. Whenever possible, they till the soil intensively.

SETTLEMENTS IN NEW YORK

The state of New York has the largest number of Ukrainian agricultural communities. Long Island is dotted with farms operated by Ukrainians, and several of their settlements are large.[9] Here their farms are small, being about 10 acres in extent, and are confined to truck crops. In spite of the size, the farms are profitable, for New York City and its suburbs furnish a ready market for fresh vegetables, fruits, and poultry in normal times.[10] Long Island potatoes are well known in the metropolis. The farmers also raise beans, beets, cucumbers, tomatoes, cabbages, parsnips, carrots, garlic, and other garden products. Large trucks come each day during the growing season to collect the produce and haul it to market. These small farmers are better off than their fellow-countrymen who work at manual labor in near-by cities, and they are well satisfied, rarely complaining. Scientific methods of farming are used whenever possible, and the Ukrainians take better care of their machinery than do the native Americans. The farmhouses do not differ from those of Americans except that flowers are grown in profusion about them. There are also a few Ukrainian communities in the central part of the state, the most important being in the vicinity of Galway, Broadalbin, Lee Center, Glenfield, Spring Valley, Hudson, and Durhamville.[11] These Ukrainians are engaged primarily in dairying and fruit-raising,[12] and their farms are much larger and more profitable than those in New England, the average being probably 90 acres. Most of the Ukrainian farming communities in New York were started during the decade 1910–20.

RURAL GROUPS IN NEW JERSEY

New Jersey has a considerable number of Ukrainian farmers in various parts of the state. The oldest rural settlement started about 1908 in the vicinity of Great Meadows. The first to go there were laborers on truck farms. Year after year, new immigrants joined them, mostly from two villages in the Ukraine, until they became quite numerous. At first they worked for wages or on a percentage basis, saved money, and eventually bought land from their American employers, gradually forcing them out of the community. The extent of this penetration is seen in the enrolment at the Alafeno rural school. As late as 1912 almost all the children were of American stock, while in 1934, out of seventy-five pupils, only one was of American ancestry, all others being children of Ukrainian and Polish immigrants.[13]

The largest colony in New Jersey is near Millville in the southern part of the state, and its story is slightly different. About 1912 a Ukrainian real estate agent named W. Metolich began to advertise land for sale in that vicinity in the *Svoboda* (Jersey City). The advertisement was so appealing, one might say sugar-coated, that its influence was felt not only in the near-by urban centers but also in faraway North Dakota. A number of Dakota farmers sold their large farms and moved to Millville, where they purchased small strips of land. Many soon became dissatisfied with their new holdings and complained that the land had been overadvertised and even misrepresented, but it was too late to mend matters.[14] About two hundred families built homes, farm buildings, two churches, and schools at Millville. After the first years of hardship they became more contented and remained. Their farms are small, being 10 or more acres in extent, but the sandy soil is productive and easily cultivated. Many of the farmers grow truck crops.[15] Nova Ukraina, near Plainfield, is the youngest Ukrainian rural community, being still in the process of settlement. In 1936 it had ten families engaged in poultry-raising.

THE MINER-FARMERS

In Pennsylvania the Ukrainian farmers are scattered.[16] Some of them are former urban residents who disliked city life and turned back to the soil. In mining regions from which the coal has been removed, the mining companies have sold land to their former workers—the Ukrainian, Slovak, and other Slavic immigrants—at a very low price.[17] Very often the growing timber was worth the price paid for the land. It supplied lumber for farm buildings, and often there was also some for sale. This sort of land is usually hilly, but many of the Ukrainians were accustomed to such topography, having come from the Carpathian region of the homeland. At first, they sought part-time work in the mines, but, as mining receded farther and farther from their homes, they had to devote their full time to farming. Through hard work by the entire family they were able to sustain themselves, and today they continue to cultivate their hilly farms intensively wherever possible and to raise cattle, hogs, and sheep. Besides these individual farmers scattered through the state, there are several large Ukrainian agricultural communities; the most noted are those at Green Hill,[18] Doylestown, Quakertown, Allentown, Sippack, and Albion, the latter having nearly seventy families.[19] The farmers of Green Hill, some sixteen families, have settled on such rocky soil that they are unable to make a living from farming alone, and so most of them try to find some type of employment in neighboring towns. In these communities nearly every farmer owns his farm, and few of them are mortgaged. The crops are widely diversified.

The Protestant refugees who fled from the province of Kiev to escape the religious persecution of Czar Alexander III and the Russian Orthodox church constitute an important as well as an interesting element of the Ukrainian immigration. Some of them came to America as early as 1885 and 1887. They worked in the manufacturing districts of Philadelphia until they had accumulated sufficient money, and then they began farming near Yale, Virginia, in 1894.[20] A number of Ukrainian farmers also settled at York, Virginia, and at Curtis Bay, Maryland. Their farms consist of 10–40 acres of partly cleared land with poultry as the chief source of income. Many of the families still rely primarily on the cities for their earnings. Several are storekeepers, bakers, and contractors.[21]

CONTRACT LABORERS ON HAWAIIAN PLANTATIONS

On several occasions emigrants from the Ukraine were headed for Canada, but, when they came to the German port from which they expected to sail, they learned that the North German Lloyd was not doing business with that country. The agents of that company, Karesz–Stotzky and Fr. Missler, dissuaded the people from going to Canada and urged them to buy tickets for other destinations instead. Thus in the autumn of 1898, some 365 men, women, and children were transported even to the Hawaiian Islands, where they were reduced to a position of servitude on the plantations. This situation was brought about by their having been persuaded, before leaving Germany, to sign contracts which they apparently did not understand. Appeal to the Austrian consul in Hawaii brought no relief as he was benefiting financially at the expense of his subjects. Finally conditions became so unbearable that they went on strike. When the news of their suffering reached the editor of the *Svoboda* paper, he wrote letters to different United States congressmen, asking them to do something about the situation. At last, through the threatened intervention of the United States government, they were set free, and several migrated at once to San Francisco.[22]

IN TEXAS AND OKLAHOMA

In 1896 a large group of Ukrainians were on their way to Canada, where they expected to take up homesteads. The steamship agents, however, persuaded them to change their plans and shipped them to Texas instead.[23] On reaching Texas the poor immigrants faced immediate disillusionment. There was no free land available. As they had to do something at once, they turned to the cotton plantations, the railroads, and the coal mines. While looking for work, they discovered Polish communities and settled near them. Since they had no ready cash to buy farms, they rented abandoned plantation land on a share basis. Most of them are still renters. The largest Ukrainian farm settlements in Texas are near Bremond, Anderson, Marlin, New Waverly, Schulenburg, and Dundee. In most of these communities they raise tobacco, cotton, and grain.[24] As there are no

Ukrainian organizations or churches among these people, they are losing their racial identity.

Many of the Ukrainians were not contented in Texas. The most frequent complaints were against the heat, the poor water, and the snakes. When Oklahoma was opened to settlement, they, in company with thousands of native Americans, rushed there, and Oklahoma now has several hundred Ukrainian farmers, the largest settlements being at Hartshorne, Harrah, and Jones.[25] Close to one hundred immigrant families settled at Hartshorne, mostly miners. Although they came from the province of Ruthenia, they have an orthodox church that is subject to the Russian bishop and, therefore, call themselves Russian. Also a considerable number of these people settled among the Czechs in their settlement, Praha. Arkansas and Missouri have a number of widely scattered Ukrainian farmers. In the latter state there are large groups in the mining region near Desloge and St. Francois.

IN MICHIGAN AND WISCONSIN

Michigan and Wisconsin have received Ukrainian farmers for nearly forty years. In Michigan the Ukrainian communities are found at Copemish, Fruitport, Pinconning, and Saline.[26] Here most of the Ukrainians bought wooded land without buildings and converted it into fruit and corn (in the American sense) farms, and there are now over two hundred families living on them. When the Ukrainians began to settle in Wisconsin in the late nineties, about the only land available at a low price was the cutover land in the northern part. They helped one another clear away the stumps and underbrush, and eventually, after years of hardship, they came to enjoy a moderate degree of prosperity. The early settlers were well to do before the depression, having large farms and spacious buildings. Altogether they number about a hundred and fifty families. In the settlements at Clayton, Lublin, and Thorp, the farms vary in size from 80 to 1,000 acres. Although the farmers here experiment with many crops, the chief income is derived from dairy products.[27] Later comers have not fared so well. After the World War many

Ukrainians left the cities and purchased farms in Ohio, Indiana, and, a few, in Illinois. The Belegay, a Ukrainian real estate agency in Chicago, placed scores of families on land in Indiana and near-by states. The depression beginning in the late twenties drove many of them from the cities.

REAR VIEW OF MODERN FARM HOME OF STANLEY OLEAS
UKRAINIAN FARMER, SOUTH RANGE, WISCONSIN

NORTH DAKOTA COMMUNITIES

The Ukrainian farm element in North Dakota has an interesting history. The members of the first group to arrive there came by way of Canada in 1896 and 1897. They had intended to settle in the Dominion, but, disliking their immediate prospects, they were persuaded by Dakota agents to try the plains. In some cases their transportation was paid. These first settlers were from East Galicia, and they settled on land that later became known as the towns of Belfield and Wilton.[28] In 1933 there were only seventeen Ukrainian families living in the town of Belfield, but the country surrounding it had two hundred and thirty-seven additional families in the communities of Ukraina, Gorham, and Snow. Ten families also settled in the vicinity of New Hradec, which is a Czech (Bohemian) community, not far from Dickinson. Ukraina seems to be the center of Ukrainian population in the southwestern part of the state. There are two attractive churches at Ukraina and a third one a few miles away at Gorham. On Sundays or on festival days, when their girls wear

PIONEER SOD HOUSE OF UKRAINIAN PRAIRIE FARMER
DMYTRO HAVRYLUK, UKRAINA, NORTH DAKOTA

national costumes, they are a picturesque group. A few Germans who live among the Ukrainians there often intermarry and attend the Ukrainian churches.

A group of the Protestant refugees already referred to met a coreligionist, a Ukrainian-German named Peter Zeller, on shipboard, who dissuaded them from going to Virginia as they had planned and took them with him to Trip, South Dakota.[29] At the close of the winter, many took trains for Harvey, North Dakota. Ten families, however, bought horses, wagons, seeds, and other necessaries to start farming in a new country, and trekked there in covered wagons, reaching their destination after plowing through mud for two weeks. They filed homestead claims in McHenry and McLean counties, and several of these pioneers, still living in Kief and its vicinity, frequently tell of the hardships of their trip and the first years in North Dakota.[30] They wrote to friends and relatives in Pennsylvania, Virginia, and the Ukraine, and as a result hundreds soon joined them, the largest number coming directly from Taraschansky County in the province of Kiev in the Ukraine. Within fifteen years the Ukrainian element rose to about eight thousand.

The climate and soil of this region resemble those of the Ukraine, and, because the land was free and there was freedom of religion, North Dakota became the haven of the Ukrainian Protestants. They settled on a strip of land about 40 miles in length and about fifteen miles in width, through which the Soo Railroad was built in 1908.[31] The population is solidly Ukrainian with only rarely a Norwegian or a German farmer. In the central-western part of the state, Ukrainian immigrants occupy about half of Billings and Dunn counties. Much smaller groups live in Williams, Barnes, Trail, and Pembina counties. In 1933 they numbered close to ten thousand. South Dakota likewise has a large Ukrainian population, but they settled among farmers of other nationalities and did not form compact groups.

Coming from the steppes of the Ukraine, these immigrants were well fitted for life on the plains of North Dakota, and it did not take them long to become accustomed to the climate and conditions there. Their first few years, as with all pioneers, were filled with hardship. When the land was hilly, the enormous deposits of drift stones had to be removed. In some regions there was trouble with the ranchers. However, endurance, hard labor, and thrift brought a measure of prosperity and progress. Sod houses were replaced by wooden structures, horses by tractors, and buggies and wagons by automobiles and trucks. Instead of their original 160-acre tracts, most Ukrainian farmers now have 320, 480, and even 640 acres. Several own three and four sections each.[32] While subduing the wilderness, these immigrants did not neglect the education of their children; neither did they limit it to the three "R's," and, consequently, they produced people prepared to hold higher positions in life.[33]

A few of the Ukrainian farmers in North Dakota and other states have sought to better themselves by turning to trade or business in near-by villages. The most common enterprises that have interested them are grain elevators, grocery and hardware stores, farm-implement shops, and, in recent years, gasoline stations. A number have been quite successful. Others have become carpenters, shoemakers, barbers, or mail carriers, each according to his taste and ability. In nearly every case they have proved capable and have made a success of their work. Probably the most successful rural business men are those at Kief, Benedict, and Max, North Dakota. In Kief, W. Bukovoy owns a grain elevator and sells farm machinery; in the same village Edward Simbalenko is selling the farm implements of the McCormick Company. There are six other business establishments in the hands of Ukrainian immigrants. At Benedict the Charchenko brothers have a very successful hardware business; while at Max, Alexey Bukovay is the wholesale-fruit dealer for that community and vicinity. Of course the success of the business men depends upon the prosperity of the customers. Therefore, if the Dakota farmers do not have their crops damaged by grasshoppers or drought, and if farm prices are high, they are able to buy more and thus stimulate business.

During the World War many of the Dakota Ukrainians moved to Canada, Oregon, and Montana. The largest and oldest Ukrainian settlement in the latter state is at Scobey. It was started by a group that came by way of Canada about 1897. There are also farming communities at Sand Creek and Larslan, and farther west, near Giltedge, several Ukrainians have ranches.[34] The church records of the Ukrainian Catholic Church at Ukraina reveal that numerous Ukrainians and those of mixed marriage live on farms in eastern Montana.[35]

The Ukrainians hold a definite place among the immigrant farm groups of the United States. There are nearly thirty-eight hundred Ukrainian families, or twenty-six thousand individuals, living in eighty-five rural communities, and about one-third as many more on widely scattered farms throughout the country. Nearly all of these communities are sufficiently large to maintain churches, schools, or other forms of social organization. The Ukrainians have sought social as well as economic progress, and its achievement is manifested by schools and some forty-nine rural churches. Most of them have desired to give their children a good education, and, as a result, many of the second and third generations are teachers, nurses, physicians, and technicians. As farmers the Ukrainians are industrious and thrifty and co-operate with their neighbors of other nationalities perhaps even better than they do with one another. Appreciating the opportunities that America offered them, they are ready to participate in all good works in the land of their adoption.

NOTES FOR CHAPTER IV

1. Most of the content of this chapter appeared in print under the title "Ukrainian Farmers in the United States," in *Agricultural History*, January, 1936. Through the kind permission of the editor, Dr. Everett E. Edwards, this material is here utilized.

2. According to the authority on Ukrainian geography, Dr. Stephen Rudnitzky, in his *Pochatkova Geografia* (Kiev, 1919), p. 82, more than eight of every ten people in the Ukraine were farmers. For a similar statement, see Emil Revyuk, *Ukraine and the Ukrainians* (Washington, D.C., 1920), p. 17.

3. The following settlements and villages have a large Ukrainian agricultural population. Connecticut: Colchester, Oxford, Orange, Willimantic; Iowa: Lovilia, Osage; Maryland: Chesapeake City, Curtis Bay; Massachusetts: Pittsfield, South Deerfield; Michigan: Copemish, Fosters, Fruitport, Pinconning, Saline; Minnesota: Barnum, Osseo, Royalton; Missouri: Desloge; Montana: Giltedge, Larslan, Sand Creek, Scobey; New Jersey: Blairstown, Great Meadows, Johnsonburg, Millville, Newton, Nova Ukraina; New York: Babylon, Broadalbin, Churchville, Durhamville, Far Rockaway, Galway, Glenfield, Hudson, Lee Center, Mattituck, Middleburg, Orient, Riverhead, Roslyn, Spring Valley, Stapleton, Troy (near Woodhaven); North Dakota: Backoo, Belfield, Benedict, Butte, Caledonia, Casselton, Douglas, Fayette, Fredonia, Fried, Fryburg, Gorham, Grassy Butte, Kief, Killdeer, Kongsberg, Makoti, Mary, Max, Oakdale, Pembina, Raleigh, Ruso, Ryder, Snowe, Ukraina, Williston, Wilton; Oklahoma: Harrah, Hartshorne, Jones, Prague; Oregon: Eugene; Pennsylvania: Albion, Allentown, Doylestown, Kimberton, Green Hill, Linfield, Northampton, Olyphant, Quakertown, Skippack, Stowe, Smithmill; Texas: Anderson, Bremond, Dundee, Marlin, New Waverly, Schulenburg; Vermont: Manchester (near), Rutland; Virginia: Yale; Washington: Cedar

* The works indicated by an asterisk are in Ukrainian.

Valley, Ravensdale; West Virginia: Wheeling (near); Wisconsin: Clayton, Cornucopia, Huron, Lublin, Suring, Thorp; Wyoming: Frontier, Rock Springs, Sublet.

4. Julian Batchinsky (*Ukrainska Immigracia w Zyedinenich Derzhavach Ameriky [Lwów, Poland, 1914], I, 167–68) recorded that the Ukrainian paper, America, No. 31 (1889), advocated the establishment of Ukrainian agricultural communities.

5. Rev. Nestor Dymtriv, in the *Svoboda (Jersey City), February 16, 1899, mentions a Ukrainian farmer whom he met in 1895 near Troy, N.Y., who had been in the United States since 1864, but he did not state if the man had lived on the farm all that time. Also, according to the Spominki Ahapia Honcharenka (Kolomea, 1894), p. 34, Honcharenko states that he purchased a farm 26 miles north of San Francisco from his fellow-countryman, Joseph Krishevsky, in 1872.

6. At first about 200 Ukrainian farmers in the South rented their farms (John Kovalsky, in the *Svoboda [Scranton], July 27, 1905, p. 7). A small number in North Dakota rent their farms, especially in the vicinity of Tower City (letter from Amelia Weshnevsky to the author, August 24, 1933).

7. Letter from Rev. Theodore Halenda to the author, March 8, 1932.

8. *Letter from Mary Pasichnyk to the author, February 8, 1932; "Ukrainians in Colchester," in Narodne Slovo (Pittsburgh), March 24, 1932; letter from Rev. Alexander Rotko to the author, June 6, 1932.

9. Lev Yasenchuk, *Za Oceanom (Lwów, 1930), pp. 131–35.

10. One farmer on a small Long Island farm sold his bean crop for $4,000 (ibid., p. 134).

11. At Durhamville they settled in a community of Hungarians. The largest settlement is near Broadalbin, where there are close to one hundred families (*Svoboda [Jersey City], May 24, 1933).

12. Letter from Wasyl Habal to the author, April 23, 1932.

13. *Svoboda (Jersey City), December 19, 1933; letter from Paul Landiak to the author, January 2, 1934. According to Landiak, the locality has close to seventy-five Ukrainian families with farms varying in size from 25 to 600 acres.

14. At a meeting in the home of N. Hevchuk on April 5, 1914, the following resolution of complaint was adopted: "1. All of us suffered due to false advertising of land in the Svoboda paper. 2. We wish to warn our fellow countrymen not to heed such false advertising and come here to buy land." It was signed by sixteen men and printed in the *Narodna Vola (Scranton), August 14, 1914.

15. Stepan Museychuk, "Impressions of Our Farm Life," in the *Svoboda (Jersey City), July 13, 1931.

16. For details on the Ukrainians of Pennsylvania in industries other than farming, see Wasyl Halich, "Ukrainians in Western Pennsylvania," Western Pennsylvania Historical Magazine XVIII (June, 1935), 139–46.

17. At first the farms consisted of 10–20 acres and they were purchased for $5.00 per acre (Batchinsky, op. cit., pp. 172–74).

18. Letter from Rev. P. Turiansky to the author, June 23, 1936.

19. The same community has Polish and Slovak farmers (letter from John J. Ulan, Jr., to the author, February 6, 1932).

20. Letter from Andrew Dubovay to the author, November 12, 1932.

21. Letter from S. C. Malin to the author, February 9, 1932.

22. *Letter from Dmytro Puchalsky to the author, October 16, 1932; a more complete account about the Ukrainian settlers in Hawaii may be found in the

Svoboda (Mount Carmel, Pa.), May 17, 1900, or in the *Almanac of the Ukrainian Workingmen's Association* (1936), pp. 80–92. Batchinsky, *op. cit.*, p. 176.

23. Some accounts state that the first group that reached Texas in 1896 consisted of sixty families; others say that there were more than a hundred. The agents transported them to the vicinity of Vernon (letter from Rev. A. Revera to the author, October 19, 1932).

24. Batchinsky, *op. cit.*, pp. 177–78.

25. The migration of the Ukrainians from Texas to Oklahoma took place in 1905–6. Today, except for the three organized communities of Harrah, Hartshorne, and Jones, most of the immigrants are widely scattered throughout the state, and they have lost nearly all of their national identity among the Poles, Czechs, and Croats (letter from Rev. A. Revera to the author, October 19, 1932).

26. Letter from Rev. Lev. J. Sembratovich to the author, March 22, 1932.

27. Wasyl Halich, "Ukrainians in Wisconsin," *Svoboda* (Jersey City), June 28, 1932.

28. At that time the land was not yet surveyed, although there was a land office at Dickinson, twenty miles east (Halich, "The Ukrainian Farmers in North Dakota," *Narodne Slovo* [Pittsburgh], December 14, 1933, and "Through the Ukrainian Villages in North Dakota," *Svoboda* [Jersey City], August 28, 1933).

29. The author is indebted for knowledge of this incident to an eyewitness, George Michalenko, who still lives at Kief, N.D.

Numerous German agricultural communities existed in the Ukraine, some of them dating from the reign of Peter the Great. By 1880 many from these communities emigrated to the Dakotas, and through them the Ukrainian Protestants learned of homesteads. In Dakota these Germans are commonly called Russians and so also, in most communities, are the Ukrainians. While visiting nearly all of the Ukrainian settlements in North Dakota, the author learned of only one real Russian farmer, and he lived north of Max. Nevertheless, one Russian author, Marko Uchimovich Vilchur, in his †*Russkie v Amerike* (New York, 1918), pp. 40–45, gave considerable space to the "Russians" of that state. Although the Germans of North Dakota emigrated from the Ukraine, they are considered as Germans in this article. Similarly the word "Russian" is used to designate a person of Russian blood, speech, and nationality, formerly called Muscovite, and more recently Great Russian, and not a person of any nationality born within the old Russian empire.

30. In 1933 five of the original group were living at Kief.

31. Letter from Edward Simbalenko to the author, January 27, 1932.

32. Letter from Rev. John Senchuk to the author, April 26, 1932.

33. In 1933 sixty-six sons and daughters of North Dakota Ukrainians were teaching, and nearly as many more had taught school (Halich, *"Ukrainian Teachers in American Schools," *Svoboda* [Jersey City], August 15, 1933).

34. In 1933 Scobey had thirty-one Ukrainian families, according to H. Kinzersky, a member of the group. A ranchman acquainted with Montana observed that many Ukrainian laborers come and go in Great Meadows, Anaconda, Butte, and Miles City (letter from Sava P. Charnecky to the author, September 18, 1932).

35. In North Dakota the Ukrainians mostly marry within their own nationality, but it is possible to find in every community some that have married Norwegians or Germans. As long as the prospective son-in-law or daughter-in-law is of good character, the Ukrainian parents in North Dakota do not object to mixed marriages.

† In Russian.

CHAPTER V

BUSINESS AND THE PROFESSIONS

BESIDES the laborer, miner, and farmer, Ukrainian immigration added business and professional men to American society. Comparatively few of the early Ukrainian immigrants had any business experience before coming to America, for their country had been ruled by foreign despots who discouraged them from such activity. Most of the business was in the hands of foreign elements—Jews, Germans, Greeks, and Russians.[1] Those immigrants who had had a limited amount of commercial training acquired it in a village or city co-operative store.[2]

THE BEGINNINGS

If a newcomer went into business in America, it was not often because of his knowledge of it, but on account of the opportunity he saw in it to better himself materially. With a few exceptions, the Ukrainian business men started at the bottom.[3] Most of them began with such simple enterprises as rooming- and boarding-houses. Owing to the fact that in the first few years of Ukrainian immigration not many immigrants brought their families along with them to America, it was natural that those who did so should be persuaded to take in roomers and boarders. Not infrequently more roomers were crowded into a house than was consistent with decent comfort—four to six men in a room, and as many as twelve in a house. Such roomers paid three to four dollars per month each; if board were included, then the prices were about four times as high. Small as it seems, such income frequently exceeded the earnings of the family man who worked in the mine or factory.[4] The wife of the immigrant, as has already been noted, overtaxed her strength by doing so much work single-handed for the sake of enlarging the family income.[5]

TYPES OF BUSINESS

For the most part the Ukrainian business enterprises in America seem to fall into the following classes: individual businesses, co-operative stores, and the management of the branch businesses of large American stores. Not many Ukrainian Americans are in partnership with one another or with Americans.

INDIVIDUAL ENTERPRISES

The Ukrainian immigrants, as a group, are noted for their industry and thrift; and so, after accumulating a small amount of capital, some of them deserted mill or mine work and started in the saloon business. A few who did this had been keepers of rooming- and boarding-houses. As the liquor business was usually a success, there was no longer need of keeping boarders; therefore the saloon-keeper's wife gained a partial relief from hard labor. For a number of years the saloon was a social center of the immigrant life. It was there the immigrant met his friends in the evening and on Saturday and exchanged news about the old country and learned of a possible opportunity of a better job in some mill. Although the vice of drunkenness was limited to week ends and paydays, a considerable amount of money was spent on liquors, and Ukrainian saloons multiplied in every town where these people lived.[6] Among their countrymen the saloon-keepers became the most prosperous group, and as such their word carried much weight in such matters as the building of churches and the appointing and transferring of priests. In spite of the fact that the saloon-keeper was not always the most ideal character, in many instances he became the most influential man in the parish, having even more influence than the priest himself.[7]

The individual enterprises include as many varieties of commerce as one finds in an average American city. Next to the saloon (now the tavern) came the grocery store. This business, as a rule, required more investment and more intelligence; it rendered smaller yield on the investment, but it was a business of sobriety. It became the most common of all Ukrainian American commercial enterprises.[8] In almost every city where these people live there are one or more grocery-meat stores. Unlike American establishments, they do not have free-delivery systems; neither are they on a cash-and-carry basis. The common practice is to pay the grocery bill on payday; the Ukrainian women call this buying "on a book." As long as the people work or have money, they pay their bills, although there are occasional exceptions. About forty-five years' experience in this business has brought some prosperity.[9] The owners of such stores are frequently the people whose children attain higher educations. Other very common business establishments are bakeries, restaurants, drug stores, and hardware and furniture stores.[10] Several restaurants are operated by Ukrainian immigrants in each of the following cities: Hartford (Connecticut), Woonsocket (Rhode Island), New York, Brooklyn, Rochester, Pittsburgh, Chicago, and Minot (North Dakota). There are also individuals who operate restaurants and summer resorts in New England communities, New York, and Pennsylvania;[11] several operate hotels. There are likewise a few coal dealers. Local opportunities determine the business pattern.

Immigrants possessing some technical skill, or who had a trade, opened barber, tailoring, shoe-repairing, and printing shops and other establishments. In nearly all instances such businesses were set up among Ukrainian and other immigrants. From such humble beginnings ambitious individuals expanded their businesses and eventually moved to better quarters. In recent years funeral homes have been established in many cities and seem to prosper, although the rate of mortality is not very high among Ukrainian Americans.[12] The following three funeral directors have large establishments: Jarema in New York City, Kania in McKees Rocks (Pennsylvania), and Jewusiak and Sons in Jersey City.[13]

Among the most successful and widely established businesses of Ukrainian Americans is that of window-cleaning. There is hardly a city in the country that does not have these enterprising Slavic people cleaning windows for the large business houses. They accept contracts for all types of buildings, and, in a few cities have a monopoly on this pursuit. According to one clergyman, the window-cleaners are the most prosperous members of his parish.[14] Even during the years of depression, one of such business men in a Texas city wrote that both he and his co-workers were doing well either in a business of their own or working for their countrymen; all owned their homes.[15] In Newark, New Jersey, one of the Ukrainian window-cleaners, Sokolovsky, after twelve years of work, purchased an apartment house for sixteen families for the price of one hundred thousand dollars. Although the purchaser did not pay the entire sum in cash, he displayed a daring business spirit.[16]

A few other types of individual enterprises that deserve special mention are the laundries, garages, gasoline stations, and confectionery stores. In the city of Newark, New Jersey, are two other successful Ukrainian business men in addition to Sokolovsky. One is operating a laundry and the other a bakery. The business of these men extends beyond the city limits to a large college several miles away from Newark.[17] One of the largest garages in Chicago is owned and operated by a Ukrainian, a man who kept a grocery store for a number of years. Several contractors and builders have well-established businesses in Newark, Cleveland, and Chicago.

In addition to the various types of enterprises already described, the book and music stores likewise deserve mention. At present only one bookstore exists that sells books alone; it is in connection with the *Svoboda*, the Ukrainian daily newspaper in Jersey City. Five other stores find it more profitable to sell music supplies, phonographs, radios, and art works along with the books.[18] One of these book and music stores, the Surma Book and Music Company of New York City, exceeds all others of its kind in volume of business. The success of this store is partly due to wide advertising in the press and over the radio. The Surma radio programs given once a week attract the attention of other than Ukrainian listeners; consequently, the proprietor receives orders from customers beyond the city limits of New York. A large percentage of the business, therefore, is through the mail. This particular establishment carries more Ukrainian phonograph records than any other store in the world.

Beginning about 1910 numerous steamship agencies were established among the Ukrainian Americans. They represented various foreign companies, mostly German. During the years when the doors of immigration were open and business flourished, those agencies not only sold steamship tickets and aided the immigrant in bringing his family to America but also sent money for the immigrants to Europe. Since the immigration traffic came to a close, many such agencies have continued to exist by selling a few tourist tickets and doing a real estate business. A few indulged in banking practices by taking charge of people's savings. Such agencies have been operated in several cases by unscrupulous men who embezzled hundreds of thousands of the immigrants' dollars.[19] Undoubtedly such dishonesty lessened the confidence of the immigrants in their own countrymen and forced them to do business with American banks, many of them only to lose their life's savings when the banks closed during the depression.

CO-OPERATIVE VENTURES

In addition to individual business enterprises, large and small, a few co-operative stores are operated by Ukrainian Americans. In 1887 Rev. Fr. Volansky was the first to establish such stores among the Ukrainians in Pennsylvania.[20] Since then, co-operatives have appeared and disappeared in large numbers. Whenever there was efficient and honest management, the stores prospered; people invested their money and heartily supported them.[21] On various occasions, however, unscrupulous newcomers, who wanted to get rich quickly at the expense of their countrymen, ruined such businesses and undermined confidence in the idea; occasionally an ignoble priest also ruined the local co-operative ventures.[22] Now and then the co-operative enterprise was purchased by one of its managers and continued in private hands. Only four such stores existed in 1936, namely, in New Britain (Connecticut), Crompton (Rhode Island), New York, and Wilkes-Barre (Pennsylvania).

Although the Ukrainian sense of individualism craves for private ownership of business, several men obtained technical business training in schools and after a brief period of apprenticeship obtained a managership of a branch office of a big corporation; others worked themselves up to such positions. Five of such men are regional representatives of the McCormick Company. Others are managing the local business in various cities for the Woolworth stores. Several men are operating company stores in Pennsylvania mining communities and lumber-yards and grain elevators in North Dakota.[23]

LARGER ESTABLISHMENTS

Ukrainian Americans have not advanced as yet in the business world to the class of big business, but several individuals are headed in that direction. To such a class belongs the immigrant, Platon Stasiuk, who twenty-one years ago started a small meat market and by 1933 had enlarged it so that it was one of the largest and best-equipped meat markets in New York City. He operates also a branch store in Brooklyn, giving employment to some forty people.[24] His business was such a success that even during the years of depression it necessitated expansion of premises and equipment at the cost of some twenty-five thousand dollars.[25] Besides Platon Stasiuk, several other immigrants have displayed superior business ability. To this group belongs Wasyl Bukovoy, of Kief, North Dakota, a grain dealer;[26] Philemon Tarnavsky, a farmer in North Dakota; Dr. Stephan Sochotzky, owner of a factory in New York City, and Igor I. Sikorsky of the Sikorsky Aviation Corporation.[27]

In 1936 no less than ten Ukrainians headed or owned manufacturing establishments. The most renowned of these enterprises was the Sikorsky Aviation Corporation, Bridgeport, Connecticut. Next to it in importance may be classed Sochotzky's Zellotone Chemical Company of New York City. Pylyp Yarosh owns a canning factory in the vicinity of Orange, Connecticut,[28] and there are also two small manufacturing establishments in the suburbs of Pittsburgh. Others consist of tailor and furrier establishments in Brooklyn (New York) and Bridgeton (New Jersey), each employing a score or more persons. Several plants have been making soda-water.

In Cleveland, Ohio, the Ukrainians organized a bakery cor-

THE INTERIOR OF ONE OF P. STASIUK'S MEAT MARKETS IN NEW YORK CITY

poration which represented an initial investment of two hundred thousand dollars. The corporation in 1933 employed forty-one people, of whom all but eleven were immigrants; eleven trucks distributed bread to five hundred stores. The average monthly business done was fifteen thousand dollars.[29] There were also two other bakeries in Cleveland operated by Ukrainian Americans.

THE INVESTMENT OF SAVINGS

From the preceding accounts it is apparent that the Ukrainian immigrants possess both industry and thrift. A pertinent and interesting question is: What do they do with their money? In reply one may say that, if there is any surplus after all the bills are paid, the Ukrainians keep their money in the banks or invest it. Ever since the United States Postal Savings Bank was established, a very large number of Ukrainians have deposited their savings there, preferring the safety of deposit assured by the government to the higher interest paid by privately owned institutions at the risk of insecurity.[30] An enterprising minority frequently organize building and loan associations, which are, as a rule, connected with some church. At present there is one in Newark, two in Pittsburgh, and one in Chicago. The organization in Newark, New Jersey, handles about a million dollars annually; some members deposit their money with the organization, while others borrow it.[31] A small number of prosperous Ukrainian business men in several cities went beyond this type of financial institution and founded banks.

THE FOUNDING OF BANKING INSTITUTIONS

The banking business in the hands of the Ukrainian Americans is a new thing, although a few individuals had worked in banks even before the World War. Most of the Ukrainian banks in America have come into existence since 1919.[32] Ukrainian groups of Cleveland, Ohio, founded two such banking institutions, both of which have survived the hard years of depression, although their resources were depleted. For example, the Ukrainian Savings Company of Cleveland had capital and deposits of $1,500,000 before the depression, but by December 31, 1931, this total had been reduced to $622,337.41.[33] However, the depositors have remained loyal and continue to patronize the institutions.[34] One of the banks in Shamokin, Pennsylvania, is also operated by Ukrainians.

ATTEMPTS AT ORGANIZATION

Since 1920 the number of Ukrainian merchants in the United States has increased. By 1931 some of these business men of large cities saw the necessity of organization for commercial as well as for civic purposes. Thus far not much has been accomplished, although in some large cities the professional men went hand in hand with the business men in order to be able to draw in others for the common purpose, but the majority are reluctant and prefer not to join. Some success has been attained in New York, where two grocery associations have been organized with a small membership; likewise in Cleveland and Chicago.[35] The business men of Newark, New Jersey, are much better organized than their neighbors in New York, having had forty members almost from the beginning. The New Jersey organization is doing relief work among the immigrants, aiding the unemployed, and occasionally financing lecture courses.[36]

THE PROFESSIONS

The first Ukrainian ever mentioned practicing a profession in the United States was Rev. A. Honcharenko, a teacher in New York from 1865 to 1867. Another early teacher of whom we have a record was D. D. Perch, who taught in the public schools of Olyphant, Pennsylvania, during the years 1895–1900.[37] Several other Ukrainians were engaged in professional practice chiefly among their own countrymen during the last two decades of the nineteenth century.

The first Ukrainian physician in the United States had an adventurous career. It was in the early eighties that Dr. N. K. Russel, who was a political refugee, fled from Kiev to San Francisco. His full name was Nikolai Konstantinovich Sudzilovsky. It was reported, however, that even before his arrival in America he used the name Russel. He practiced medicine in San Francisco until about 1895, when he went to Hawaii. In 1896 he aided in organizing a Hawaiian medical society, and when the islands became a part of the United States, he became a leader of the native party that wanted self-government. Dr. Russel was elected to the senate and on February 10, 1901, was made the presiding officer, but he resigned from the vice-presidency and the senate on April 10 of the same year. Though he did not stay long in the legislature, he was instrumental in passing a homestead law, by which many landless families benefited, among them three hundred and sixty-five Ukrainian (Galician) immigrants, who obtained land near Mountain View. After he abandoned politics, Dr. Russel continued to practice medicine at Hilo and Olaa, in the vicinity of which he owned a plantation. About 1909 he emigrated to Nagasaki, Japan, and, according to the latest report, he died in Tientsin, China, in 1931.[38]

Ukranian Americans of professional training may be divided into two groups: those who received a part or the whole of their education abroad and those of American training. The former group consists of some three hundred and twenty-five clergy of various sects, about three hundred *diaks* (teachers and choir directors), also several lawyers, doctors, and all the newspapermen. The latter group includes the teachers in the American schools, numerous technical experts, and most of the lawyers, doctors, and all the dentists.[39] Those who work altogether among the immigrants are people who, as a rule, think in a European way and tend to devote most of their attention to the problems abroad. It is only since the World War that they have begun to take more interest in American life. Poland, through her cruelty to the Ukrainian people in the provinces that were given her by the Allied Powers, did more to create American-minded citizens out of Ukrainian immigrants than any other single factor in the entire history of immigration.[40]

NUMBERS ENGAGED IN PROFESSIONAL WORK

It is soon discovered that the number of professional men and women among the Ukrainian Americans is not large in proportion to the population. This fact is due to the economic condition of the immigrant. A majority of all the men of the first generation who completed their education in the United States had to work their way through school. The children and grandchildren of the immigrants have had an easier time; their education for the most part has been financed by parents and other relatives, or through scholarships.[41] The closest investigation, although not complete, reveals that in 1937 the following numbers of Ukrainian blood were professionally engaged: sixty-one doctors, eighteen dentists, sixty-eight lawyers, thirty-four engineers, twenty-five journalists, twenty-six druggists, one West Point graduate army officer, and sixty-six graduate nurses. Adding to these six hundred and twenty-five clergymen and choir directors, two hundred and sixty-two teachers (including two in Hawaii and one in Alaska), and twenty-one bankers, one achieves a total of twelve hundred and seven. There is also a score of accountants, clerks in banks, and agricultural experts. The number of these people professionally engaged is far too inadequate to serve the needs of the immigrants, who seem to feel more at ease with their own professional men than with those of foreign blood. Doctors and dentists who understand the language of their ancestors find it very useful in their practice. If in a certain town there are no Ukrainian professional men, these immigrants seem to have the highest confidence in Germans and Americans. The expected professional increase will come from numerous young people now in training schools and universities, provided they will not open up their offices strictly among the "Americans of old stock."[42] In the past it was the Jews who spoke Ukrainian who capitalized upon this opportunity and catered to a Ukrainian clientele.

Those men and women whose profession of necessity takes them among Americans include the teachers in various schools, from the one-room rural school in North Dakota to the state universities; also some of the nurses, engineers, technical experts, journalists, and artists. Out of a fairly large number engaged in education, the following deserve special consideration: Captain John Barabash, music, Harrison High School, Chicago; Drs. Vladimir P. Timoshenko, department of economics, Stephen

ALEXANDER ARCHIPENKO, UKRAINIAN SCULPTOR
Born May 30, 1887, at Kiev, Ukraine

Timoshenko, department of engineering, and Andrew Uchenko, department of philosophy—all of the University of Michigan; Drs. Alexander Granovsky[43] and N. Haidak, both of the School of Agriculture, University of Minnesota; and Dr. G. Potapenko, department of physics, California Institute of Technology. In the field of music an outstanding name is that of Alexander Kochetz, known throughout Europe and America as a composer and director. Kochetz is introducing Ukrainian music to the American public.[44] There are also numerous independent music teachers in large cities. Roman Prydatkevich and Michael Hayvoronsky are two young gifted musician-composers, both of whom obtained their musical education in Europe. They live in New York City, where they give lessons on stringed instruments. A considerable number of professional singers of secondary importance travel all over the country with numerous "Russian" musical organizations and appear on the programs; a few sing in New York operas. A Ukrainian opera company consisting mostly of operatic singers of experience met with much success during the winter season of 1933–34 presenting Ukrainian operas in different large cities.[45] In the field of art the Ukraine's greatest contribution to America is Alexander Archipenko, the eminent sculptor and painter.[46] Among the younger group born in America, one of the most promising is Maria Nahirna, a commercial artist, whose work appears elsewhere in this volume. This, it may be assumed, is but the beginning of the professional and cultural contribution of the Ukrainian Americans. Much is expected of them in the future, especially in the fields of music, art, and science.

NOTES FOR CHAPTER V

1. Stephan Rudnitzky, *Pochatkova Geografia* (Kiev, 1919), pp. 96–99.

2. By 1914 the entire country was covered with small co-operative organizations. On January 1, 1914, there were in the Ukraine (under Russia) 6,510 co-operatives (Emil Revyuk, *Trade with Ukraine* [Washington, D.C., 1920], p. 9).

3. Rev. Agapius Honcharenko, having lived in England and Egypt for many years as a political refugee, learned the English language. Within two years after his arrival in America he was publishing a newspaper in San Francisco (1867–71).

4. Julian Batchinsky, *Ukrainian Immigration in the United States* (Lwów, 1914), pp. 185–86.

* The works indicated by an asterisk are in Ukrainian.

5. Similar conditions prevailed among many other recent immigrants from southeastern Europe.

6. Although not many Ukrainian immigrants became habitual drunkards, they drank on all occasions, social and otherwise; the only ones that did not drink at all (as a rule) were the farmers, Protestants, and the saloon-keepers (Ivan Ardan, "The Ukrainians in America," *Charities* XIII [1904–5], 246–52).

7. Batchinsky, *op. cit.*, pp. 187–89.

8. The common evidence is the city of Carteret, New Jersey. Out of twelve advertisements that appeared in the Ukrainian monthly, seven were those of grocery stores (*Ukrainian Herald* [Carteret], August, 1933).

9. The first grocery stores were founded in Shenandoah, Pennsylvania, and vicinity, by Rev. John Volansky. In 1934 about two thousand grocery stores in some two hundred and fifty communities were operated by the Ukrainians.

10. The first hotel-keeper was Michael Halaiko, in Geneva, New York. His business was advertised in the *Svoboda* (Mount Carmel, Pa.), March 11, 1897. In 1904 three Ukrainians operated hotels and two operated summer-resort businesses.

11. *Letter from Rev. Joseph Zelechivsky (Boston) to the author, July 9, 1931; letter from Rev. Theodore Halenda (Hartford) to the author, March 9, 1932.

12. A great majority of them came to America after 1900 and were very young at the time of their arrival.

13. Jarema's of East Seventh Street in New York City is about as large as the Ukrainian church that is directly across the street from it; Kania's of McKees Rocks has a branch office in Pittsburgh. The establishment "Jewusiak and Sons" of Jersey City also operates funeral homes in Passaic and Bayonne (*Almanac of Sojedinenija* [Homestead, Pa., 1930], p. 158).

14. *Letter from Rev. Humphrey Kovalsky to the author, March 2, 1932.

15. *Letter from D. Kuritza to the author, December 28, 1932.

16. *Svoboda* (Jersey City), April 18, 1924.

17. The Shkira Bakery of Newark supplies Rutgers University at New Brunswick, New Jersey (*Svoboda* [Jersey City], September 9, 1933).

18. Other Ukrainian book and music stores are located in the cities of New York, Newark, Philadelphia, Pittsburgh, and Detroit.

19. To this group of men belongs a certain Choma, formerly of Pittsburgh, and Klem, of Chicago.

20. See chap. iii, p. 29.

21. In 1919, co-operative Ukrainian stores that were doing a good business existed in the following towns of Connecticut: Ansonia, Shelton, Hartford, New Haven, Derby, Meriden, and Terryville. The total capital invested amounted to $63,095.76. Several other stores existed in Wilmington (Del.) and Newark (N.J.) (W. Sklaryk, "Ukrainian Co-operative Stores in the United States," *Narodna Vola* [Scranton, Pa.], May 19, 1919).

22. The most successful Ukrainian co-operative stores in America were the ones founded by Rev. John Volansky in Shenandoah, Pennsylvania, and vicinity. They lasted only three years, however, because of the recall of Volansky to the Ukraine, and the ruinous policy of his successor, Father Andruchovich (letter from Rev. John Ortinsky [Shenandoah] to Rev. Alex Prystay, May 12, 1930).

23. In 1934 no less than fifteen such men were known to the author; they were widely scattered through the country east of the Rocky Mountains.

24. Stasiuk's stores are located at 124 Fifth Street, New York, and 628 Fifth Avenue, Brooklyn (*Svoboda* [Jersey City], November 24, 1933). Good accounts of this business may be found in the *National Provisioner* (Chicago), April 23, 1932, pp. 46–47, and in the *Butcher's Advocate* (New York), February 15, 1932.

25. A complete description of the business place is given in the *Svoboda* (Jersey City), October 9, 1933; also in the *National Provisioner*, November 9, 1935, p. 46.

26. Mr. Bukovoy is the owner of a grain elevator, farm-implement store, and a gasoline station.

27. Mr. I. I. Sikorsky comes from a noted Ukrainian family of clergymen in Kiev, Ukraine (letter from I. I. Sikorsky to the author, August 30, 1933).

28. Dr. S. Sochotzky, the owner of the radium factory, was also, in 1921, the president of the Ukrainian Bank in New York (*Svoboda* [Jersey City], February 5, 1921; letter from Rev. Alexander Rotko to the author, June 6, 1932).

29. Letter from William Volansky, Mgr., to the author, March 18, 1933.

30. The act of Congress, June 25, 1910.

31. Dr. Simen Dimidchuk, "Beginning of Ukrainian Immigration in America," *Almanac of the Providence Association* (Philadelphia, 1932), pp. 110–11.

32. Six such banks were in existence in 1931 in the following cities: New York, Wilkes-Barre, Shamokin, Cleveland (2), and McKees Rocks.

33. This is according to the financial statement of the Ukrainian Savings Company, Cleveland, Ohio, for December 31, 1931.

34. According to the investigation of Anna Gatz the following business enterprises were carried on by the Ukrainians in Cleveland in 1934:

Bakery	1	Florists	1
Banks	2	Funeral directors	2
Barber shops	10	Hardware stores	2
Contractors	5	Plumbers	3
Creameries and confectioneries	15	Printing company	1
Dairy companies	1	Restaurants	5
Dry cleaning and tailoring	5	Shoemakers	6
Garage	1		—
Grocery and meat markets	15	Total	75

(Letter from Anna Gatz to the author, January 25, 1934.)

35. *Svoboda* (Jersey City), February 24, 1934.

36. "Union of the Ukrainian Business Men," *Svoboda* (Jersey City), March 15, 1933. At one time fifty-three members belonged to the organization, but during the years of depression the number diminished (letter from Charles Hapanovicz to the author, May 24, 1934.)

37. Letter from D. D. Perch to the author, October 12, 1932.

38. Y. Chyz, *Almanac of the Ukrainian Working Men's Association* (Scranton, 1936), pp. 84–86. Part of this information was taken from the article of Lillian Shrewbury Merick in the *Paradise of Pacific*, January, 1912, pp. 33–39; Chyz, *ibid.*, 1937, p. 142.

39. In 1933–34 no less than 146 people from Ukrainian homes taught school in the United States.

40. See Revyuk, *Polish Atrocities in Ukraine* (New York, 1931).

41. In some cases the scholarship was awarded for high scholastic standing; in other cases for athletic ability.

42. A small number have already started medical offices, exclusively among the Americans. To such a group belong two doctors in Illinois, one in Colorado, one in

Washington, D.C., one in New York City, and to this group may also be added a druggist in North Dakota.

43. All mentioned are immigrants who made good in America. John Barabash made an excellent record as a bandmaster in a Chicago school and is a composer; Dr. Timoshenko, an authority in economics; Dr. Granovsky is listed in *Who's Who in Science*.

44. He first gained fame as a director of the Ukrainian National Chorus with which he traveled (1919–23) in Western Europe and America, including the United States and Mexico. In 1933 the Witmark Educational Publications accepted his composition of Ukrainian songs for publication (*Svoboda* [Jersey City], January 19, 1933). His English arrangements of Ukrainian folk songs are becoming popular in American public schools. Mr. Koshetz is now an American citizen.

45. Philip Becker Goez, a music critic, who witnessed the presentation of Ukrainian operas thus described it: "The first American performance of Tchaikowsky's opera 'Mazeppa,' was given last Saturday at Mecca Temple in New York. The director, Dimitri Chutro, with notable assistance from conductor, singers, and stage designers, covered himself with glory. Not only was the music a constant delight, but the enthusiasm of the whole cast was soon caught by the audience of 3,000, nearly all of whom were Ukrainians, whose dream of freedom is kept fresh by this story of a hero born 300 years ago" (*Evening News* [Buffalo], February 11, 1933).

46. After seeing some of Archipenko's works exhibited in the Ukrainian pavilion at the Century of Progress (1933), Inez Cunningham wrote: "Name any half-dozen sculptors the world has produced since Rodin, and you'll have to include Archipenko. Malloi will be in the list and Epstein—they like Archipenko, without argument" (*Chicago Herald and Examiner*, June 7, 1933). C. J. Bulliet's criticism of Archipenko's work: "While Archipenko is one of the three of our greatest 'modern' sculptors, he is curiously enough, an American best seller. More than 200 of his sculptures are owned in America by collectors from the Atlantic to the Pacific, in addition to numerous paintings and drawings. . . . . Archipenko is a native Ukrainian, born in Kiev, in 1887. He became a United States citizen in 1928" (*Chicago Daily News*, August 19, 1933).

Outside of the United States Archipenko's work may be found in twenty-eight art museums in the world. Besides the museums, numerous private individuals are the possessors of his works of art; among them a Swiss financier, George Falke, heads the list with forty articles (Dr. L. Myshuha, *Svoboda* [Jersey City], December 19, 1933).

CHAPTER VI

ORGANIZATIONS

FIRST UNITS OF ORGANIZATION

I T TOOK about a score of years after their arrival in the United States before the Ukrainian immigrants began to organize themselves into societies of their own. The first units to be created were the churches, and in connection with them, in the course of time, other institutions came into existence. Clergymen frequently served either as actual initiators of new activities or as directors of others in their creative work. The church buildings have, for the most part, served as meeting places for these various social units.

RUSSIAN AND UKRAINIAN FACTIONS

From the very beginning of Ukrainian organized life in America to the present time there have been two chief parties or factions that dominated immigrant activities. One of them represented independent Ukrainian nationalism and the other, being stimulated by funds from Russia, was pro-Russian.[1] To be sure, there have been numerous other factions, but these two groups have been the strongest and the most influential. Most of the leaders and the followers of these two parties came from that part of the Ukraine that was subject to Austria-Hungary until 1918; thus those who were influenced by Russian propaganda never tasted the oppression of the czarist or the Bolshevik regime. Russian propaganda among these people, both in Europe and in America, confused many, especially the poorest mountaineers of the Carpathian region. They became ready converts of the idea that their salvation rested with Russia. It is no secret that, owing to poverty, ignorance, and the confusion created by the Russian agents, many did not know of what nationality they really were. Needless to say, the two political groups, both in Europe and in America, have been hostile toward each other, although their language, religion, occupations, and pattern of society are the same.

THE BENEVOLENT ASSOCIATIONS

The study of institutional life of Ukrainian Americans reveals that among their numerous organizations the most important are the benevolent societies, the so-called "mutual aid associations." The idea itself is not of Ukrainian origin; other Slavic immigrants had benevolent societies before the Ukrainians constituted theirs. A considerable percentage of Ukrainian immigrants, their children, and grandchildren belong to one of ten existing associations. The Ukrainian Nationalist party succeeded in organizing and maintaining the following mutual aid associations: the Ukrainian National Association, the Ukrainian Workingmen's Association, the Providence, the Ukrainian Aid Association, and the Concord Association.

MEMBERSHIP AND ASSETS

A closer examination of these institutions renders some interesting facts. The Ukrainian National Association is the largest; it has its main office in its own building in Jersey City, New Jersey, and four hundred branches or units scattered throughout some fifteen states. In its building are also housed a bookstore and the facilities for the publication of the *Svoboda* daily in Ukrainian and a supplementary *Ukrainian Weekly* in English. Until the years of industrial depression this organization also published almanacs annually.[2] The depression likewise had its effect on the growth of the organization. At the close of February, 1937, it had 21,996 adult members and 8,376 children, a total of 30,372. It also reported assets (according to the annual statement at the close of 1936) of $4,402,265.40. The adult members were insured for a total of about $18,000,000. The largest number of members, according to their ages, consisted of those that were thirty-nine, forty, and forty-one. In 1935, 213 adult members died, the heaviest toll (118) being in the age group forty-five to fifty-five.[3]

HEADQUARTERS OF THE UKRAINIAN NATIONAL ASSOCIATION

Jersey City, New Jersey

The Ukrainian Workingmen's Association has its head office in Scranton, Pennsylvania. It publishes a triweekly paper, *Narodna Vola*, in Ukrainian with an extra page in English for its junior members. Even during the depression it continued to publish almanacs. In October, 1936, this organization had 9,892 adult members and 2,109 children, a total of 12,001. Its assets totaled $2,036,685.99.[4] The Providence is a Catholic organization with its head office in Philadelphia. In December, 1936, it had a total of 9,288 members and assets of $848,645.86. The National Aid Association of Pittsburgh and the Concord of Olyphant, Pennsylvania, are smaller institutions. The former had, at the close of 1936, a membership of 4,789 and assets close to $400,000, and the latter, in 1932, 2,542 members and assets of $115,639.95.[5] Each one of these associations publishes a newspaper in Ukrainian. The grand total membership of all five associations was in 1936 about 59,000 and the wealth close to $8,000,000. Although the membership has not increased during the last six years, the wealth has continued to climb in total.

ASSOCIATIONS OF THE PRO-RUSSIAN FACTION

The Russian faction of the Ukrainian immigrants in America has five benevolent associations, all but one of which have their headquarters in Pennsylvania. The Sojedinenije, of Homestead, is the largest with about 33,000 members and assets amounting (in 1935) to $7,800,000. It publishes a weekly, the *Amerikansky Russky Viestnik*, in Ukrainian dialect and the *American Russian Falcon* in English.[6] Its neighbor and competitive organization is the Sobranie at McKeesport. In 1935 it had about 14,000 members and assets of $642,612.95; its organ is a weekly, *Prosvita*, which is published in Ukrainian.[7] The Russian Brotherhood Organization of the United States is located in Philadelphia. In 1935 it had 17,513 members, a third of whom were children; its wealth was close to $1,500,000.[8] It publishes a weekly, *Pravda*, in mixed Russian and Ukrainian. The smallest of these so-called "Russian" organizations are the Russian Brotherhood Society at Wilkes-Barre and the Lemko of New York City. No official data could be obtained from these organizations, but reliable information concerning the former revealed a membership of 7,660 and assets of $825,000. All five of them had in 1935, no doubt, over 72,000 members and a wealth of more than $10,000,000.

Thus a grand total of about 131,000 Ukrainian Americans are insured in their own mutual aid associations, the wealth of which, in 1936, was close to $20,000,000. In addition to these, numerous individuals in large cities insure themselves in American insurance companies, several of which employ successful Ukrainian agents for this purpose.

THE DEVELOPMENT OF THE UKRAINIAN NATIONAL ASSOCIATION

Since there is a close resemblance between all the Ukrainian mutual aid associations, a history of one would reveal the general character of them all. The Ukrainian National Association had its birth in 1893 in Shamokin, Pennsylvania. Four clergymen were mostly responsible for its establishment; they were Hrihorey Hrushka, of Jersey City, Ivan Constankevich, of Shamokin, Teofan Obushkevich, of Olyphant, and Amvrosey Polansky, of Pittsburgh.[9] The first seven years of its existence only the adults belonged to it and paid fifty cents a month. Out of this fund a small death benefit was paid, hardly enough, however, to cover funeral expenses. Then the fee was raised to seventy cents. With the annual influx of Ukrainian immigrants, the membership also increased, and there then developed a necessity for a more scientific insurance system. Therefore, after several reorganizations at different times, this institution—as well as all other similar Ukrainian organizations—inaugurated modern insurance practices. They offer nearly as many different kinds of policies as an average American insurance company, insuring men, women, and children that are insurable. The largest number of policies issued are for $1,000.[10] With the exception of the Ukrainian National Association and the Lemko, all other of these organizations have their head offices in Pennsylvania, where the largest percentage of these people have settled, but their branch offices are located in many parts of the country. During the first forty years of its existence the Ukrainian National Association paid more than $3,250,000 in death benefits as well as contributed many thousands of dollars to various good çauses.[11]

EARLY RESTRICTIONS

During the first few years of their existence, several Ukrainian benevolent organizations restricted their membership to those of their own nationality, particularly to those that were of the Greek Catholic religion. As they increased in membership and wealth, they also broadened their principles, but even today most of them still specify that an applicant must be of Slavic ancestry and of certain religion. There are three that admit new members regardless of their religion or nationality, but on the whole, it is the Ukrainians that belong to these associations, and only rarely does one find an American or person of other nationality who joins them.

GOVERNMENT

The government of these benevolent societies, both local and national, is democratic. As a rule, the officers of the local branches are elected every year and serve gratis. The local units that have the required minimum membership are entitled to send a delegate to a quadrennial convention, his expenses being paid by the association. At such national conventions the executive officers give reports of their activities, which are open to the criticism of the delegates. The national convention is the supreme body, having the power to change the by-laws, elect all the high officers, including, in some cases, the editors, and specify their salaries. To meet the urgent problems of the organizations, the governing officials meet annually and attempt to settle those within their power. The local branches have their meetings each month. Each member must be present and pay his fee; absentees are fined. These meetings are held mostly in the church buildings immediately after morning services and very often last for hours. Occasionally they become very lively. It seems that the American-born members are not so argumentative as their fathers born abroad.

BENEFITS TO MEMBERS

Besides the various types of insurance protection, the fraternal orders give something to their members that no insurance company can give. Owing to the fact that they do not maintain high-salaried officials, they are able to save money. Various funds exist to which each member contributes a few cents a month. These special funds finance the publication of papers, almanacs, and, occasionally, books, and provide for convention expenses, aid for the orphans, the sick, and the needy. Out of the national fund a few scholarships are paid annually to aid the sons and daughters of the needy members;[12] out of the same funds various Ukrainian philanthropic institutions and indigent persons in Europe and some in America receive aid. Besides aiding their own members, some of these benevolent societies subsidize extensively various cultural institutions in Western Ukraine that are persecuted by the Polish police, army, or the (*Strzelcy*) legioners.[13] Whenever there was a chief convention of one of these organizations in the post-war years, ordinarily there was a representative of some society of East Galicia "to greet them," i.e., to ask for funds; and the ever-generous Ukrainian Americans have always responded heartily on such occasions. At the convention of the Ukrainian National Association, which was held in Detroit in 1933, $9,855 was voted to various needy causes.[14] Occasionally a well-managed local unit has the funds to be of much service to its members. Probably the best example of this type is the St. Stephen's branch, unit 221, of the foregoing association, in Chicago. During the twenty-five years of its existence it helped its members to the extent of $8,236 and donated to various other worthy causes an additional $6,639.60, a total of $14,875.60.[15] The significance of the work done by these organizations cannot be overestimated; its value has been abundantly demonstrated during the years of industrial depression, thousands of members having been aided who otherwise would have become burdens to their communities.

EFFORTS TO ENROL THE YOUTH

In recent years the serious-minded adult members of the benefit associations have become uneasy in regard to the future of their organizations. All the associations have been staging membership drives, with not very gratifying results. The ranks of the immigrants are getting thinner, and no new immigrants are coming in to take the place of those that have passed away.

The self-sacrificing parents insure their children, occasionally as many as five in one family, but when the time comes that the children become of age and are qualified to join the ranks of the adults, they either do not join at all or manifest indifference in numerous cases and drop out. The adults are perplexed at the indifference of the American-born youth to such worthy institutions. The depression only partly excuses the youth; the experience of life, no doubt, will create in them the ability to evaluate such things. Although during the post-war depression the membership of the Ukrainian benevolent societies was greatly depleted, they met the many appeals for help both here and abroad and survived.

THE OBYEDNANIA

Alongside the benevolent associations is the Obyednania (United Ukrainian Organizations), an authoritative organization that speaks in behalf of all the Ukrainian Americans. It was created after the World War, when there was much need for such a body. Very often it has had the necessity of straightening incorrect reports about the conditions in the Ukraine that came from Bolshevik of Polish sources. In behalf of the Ukrainian Americans it sent numerous telegrams to the United States government, the League of Nations, and other governments of the world, especially in the years 1930–34, protesting against the inhuman conditions in the Ukraine imposed by foreign despots.

FUNCTIONS OF THE OBYEDNANIA

The Obyednania is a civic body to which many local units in several states intrust the work that is impractical and more costly if carried on by the local groups. One of its chief functions is to collect money from the Ukrainian Americans for the purpose both of helping in the movement for the liberation of the land of their birth and of helping the needy institutions that are now persecuted by the Polish officials. During the thirteen years of its existence it has sent to Europe $254,266.68.[16] Small as the sum appears, spread over so many years, it represents the self-sacrificing spirit of the emigrants who are anxious to alleviate the distress and promote the freedom of the land of their fathers. The money comes from private individuals as well as from local organizations. Several days during the year are known among the Ukrainians in America as "days of contribution for the old country." As a matter of fact, there hardly is a public gathering at which money is not collected for some worthy cause. These people are so anxious to help their needy brethren across the sea that they neglect their own institutions in America. The leaders in Europe, however, do not always appreciate these contributions. The following reveal their attitude in writing: Urko Horonenko, "It is the holy duty of Ukrainians in America to help their Native Land with all their might"; Dr. Kyrylo Trylovsky, "Immigration is significant to the extent it helps the Native Land to its cultural, economical, and primarily political freedom."[17] Lev Yasinchuk, on the other hand, who was in America on two occasions to collect money, understands the immigrants and is ever ready to defend them. He speaks not of their "holy duty" but of their helping because of their great patriotism.[18] The following institutions and groups in Western Ukraine have been receiving help from America: the private schools (where the teaching of Ukrainian is permitted), Ukrainian war invalids, political prisoners, museums, indigent authors, and local educational societies.[19] The largest proportion of money collected in America, however, is being used to finance the movement for the liberation of the Ukraine. But in time of distress in America this organization has rendered a helping hand. During the period of floods in the spring of 1936 it appealed for funds and saw to it that they were justly and speedily distributed among the needy.

Besides handling the finances, the Obyednania frequently furnishes speakers in either English or Ukrainian for public meetings. It also takes much interest in organizing the children of the immigrants. Occasionally it publishes books or pamphlets. In 1930, when letters from Western Ukraine brought news of Polish punitive military expeditions and terrible atrocities committed by the Polish army against the Ukrainian civilians, and no foreign correspondent was able to get the facts because of the vigilant Polish police and spy system, the officials of the Obyednania sent the editor of the *Svoboda* to carry on the investigation. The United Organizations financed the project and published a book of facts.[20]

THE SMALLER ORGANIZATIONS

I. CITIZENS' CLUBS

There are several lesser organizations, often of local character, to which thousands of the Ukrainian Americans belong. Since the World War a considerable number of citizens' clubs have been organized; occasionally they are known as Democratic, because of their affiliation with that party. The membership consists of American citizens, by birth or naturalization, of both sexes. Some of these clubs are of no civic value whatsoever, their meeting places more or less resembling saloons; others are of civic importance and good influence. It is the latter type that deserves consideration. Their program is of a political and social nature. Probably the most valuable service they can render is the aiding of the immigrants in acquiring American citizenship. The more intelligent members of these clubs are good American patriots; they not only participate in the elections but are ready individually or in groups to participate in other constructive community activities. The clubs of the state of Connecticut are about the best organized. In Philadelphia several have their own buildings.[21] There is much possibility for a development of these organizations, for they are still in the stage of infancy.

II. THE UKRAINIAN WOMEN'S LEAGUE

The Ukrainian women in America in the past have belonged to the same fraternal benevolent associations as their husbands. The effort to organize them into separate social units dates to 1905, when they held the first convention, but not much was accomplished until 1925, when a group in New York City became organized. This local unit has been very active and has used its influence in creating similar clubs in the cities of other states. In 1932 a national convention was held in New York, at which forty-three societies from various cities were represented. The aims of the organization, as expressed in its constitution and the resolutions of the convention, are civic, educational, and philanthropic.[22] They seek, first of all, to help their own needy members, then aim to educate their children to be good Ameri-

HAND-DECORATED UKRAINIAN EASTER EGGS

A seasonal Ukrainian folk art that dates back to antiquity. Each district of the Ukraine has its own design and favorite color combinations. Some Ukrainian American women are very skilful in the execution of this Old World art, among them Mrs. Mary Procai, of Minneapolis, whose work is shown above.

can citizens, and to promote the social and intellectual improvement of immigrant women—by frequent lectures on hygiene, sanitation, literature, and art. The members also attempt to preserve and perpetuate the Ukrainian handicrafts. They teach the art of embroidery to their American-born daughters. In Carnegie, Pennsylvania (in 1932), Mrs. Kutcher, the wife of the Ukrainian Orthodox priest, organized a hundred and twenty-five girls of the congregation; they met on Thursdays to study Ukrainian literature, history, geography, and embroidery.[23] Another example of the activities of the Ukrainian Women's League is its participation in international art exhibits in large cities, at which the Ukrainian exhibitors always receive high prizes for handwork.[24] For several months in 1933 the organization published a literary magazine, *Zinochy Svit* ("Woman's World"), in Pittsburgh but was unable to carry on the financial burden because of a limited membership and because a large percentage of the organization funds were sent to the Ukraine. As the Ukrainian women in America are preoccupied with their domestic work and are conservative in character, they do not take much interest in their own organization. Consequently the leaders of this league meet with the obstacle of indifference.

III. THE SEECH POLITICAL GROUP

Just as the Ukrainian immigrant women are not interested in organizations, their husbands, brothers, and sons often take too much interest. They not only belong to several of them but wish to create a few more units. Therefore, when the benevolent associations attempted in 1934–35 to combine some of the local branches of their organizations for the sake of economy, they found the task difficult. A similar situation occasionally exists among the younger people. The Seech athletic organization was one unit up to about 1920. It had close to three hundred branches in several states and owned a building in Chicago in which it published a weekly paper, the *Seech*. Since then the organization has been broken up into three factions by newly arrived politicians from Europe. Although there is no necessity of mixing European politics with physical education among the Ukrainian Americans, nevertheless some individuals did not see it that way and, by doing so, damaged the organization. There are now two factions of democratic elements and one monarchical; the latter advocates monarchist principles for the Ukraine and wishes

General Paulo Skoropadsky, at one time a figurehead ruler of that country, to become its future king.[25] It is needless to say that not many Ukrainians or their American-born children have any love for monarchical ideas. Therefore, the Seech organization has suffered from uninvited political propaganda.

There are several political organizations whose sole aim it is to help the movement for the resurrection of independent Ukraine. The leading two are the O.D.V.U. (Organization for the Resurrection of the Ukraine) and the L.V.U. (League for the Liberation of Ukraine). There are a few other smaller groups in several large cities, all of which are attempting to enlist Ukrainian Americans to support this cause morally and financially.

IV. THE PROFESSIONAL GROUP

In 1933, during Ukrainian Week at the World's Fair in Chicago, about forty of the Ukrainian professionalists of the United States and Canada met and organized. Only those individuals who hold standard college degrees are eligible for membership. They have held annual meetings since then, in the same cities, places, and at the same time as the conventions of the Ukrainian Youth League. At such conventions papers are read, speeches delivered, and resolutions adopted. The group has some worthy aims but no available funds to carry them out. The chief point of discussion at the convention in 1935 was the creation of a Ukrainian academy of science in America; Dr. Alexander Sushko, then of the University of Chicago, was the advocate of the idea. In the autumn of 1935 this organization published a report of its meetings and an incomplete list of Ukrainian American college graduates.[26]

V. AVRAMENKO'S SCHOOL OF FOLK DANCING

The most interesting development that started about 1925 has been the youth movement. The first to succeed in organizing the American-born young people was a newly arrived immigrant, Vasile Avramenko, the folk-dancing instructor. He, more than anyone before him, was able to bring together the youth of Ukrainian parentage. Though he did not know any English, they understood his Ukrainian because they wanted to understand it: they loved his art. In three or four years after his arrival on American shores young Avramenko had organized and trained the children—ages six to twenty—in numerous American cities. He taught them the historic dances of the Ukraine, which

VASILE AVRAMENKO

created much interest among the young people. As soon as his pupils learned the intricate steps, they put on the colorful national costumes and appeared at first before the Ukrainian, and then before the American, public.[27] Their services are much in demand as amateur entertainers, and their public appearances have won them many prizes in contests with other national groups in several large cities.

The biggest public performance of Avramenko's Dancing School took place in 1931 in the Metropolitan Opera House in New York, with some three hundred dancers participating. It was acclaimed by the press as one of the outstanding musical performances of the year.[28] Mr. Avramenko is a very active man and able to lead the youth along his line of activity. He and his American-trained instructors have carried on this work even to the plains of North Dakota. There is hardly any Ukrainian entertainment in any large city in which the Avramenko pupils do not appear. Along with Ukrainian singing groups they also often participate in American charity programs, as well as at various public celebrations. Mr. Avramenko recently became interested in film work and organized a corporation (Avramenko Film Productions, Inc.) which produced, in 1936, the first Ukrainian talking picture in America, "Natalka Poltavka," or "The Girl from Poltava." The instructors that he trained have been carrying on the work in folk dancing that he began.

VI. UKRAINIAN YOUTH LEAGUE

Once the youth movement started, it spread extensively. The Ukrainian National Association has in its membership the largest number of young people—close to ten thousand. It publishes books and the *Ukrainian Weekly*, a supplement to the *Svoboda* daily, for them in English. Through this paper the young people are able to learn about one another in different states. Under the auspices of the Obyednania organization and the *Svoboda* paper the young people became organized in 1933 into the Ukrainian Youth League of North America. They hold annual conventions in which they actively participate. To encourage more serious thought and activity, the benevolent associations to which most of them belong offer at least once each year some literary prizes. It is surprising that the youth organization has succeeded much better in its development and activity than its senior counterpart, the Ukrainian Professionalists, that came into being at the same time.

VII. OTHER YOUTH GROUPS

There are also independent local social groups among the young people in large cities. Thus in New York there is the

Ukrainian Cultural Center, which holds an important place in social activity. Its members even publish a little almanac. In Pittsburgh and New York, university students are organized into student clubs and, in the former, publish a paper. The groups in Chicago and Detroit also publish junior papers in English. Some of the Ukrainian Orthodox churches maintain independent clubs for their young people and publish an English section for them in the *Ukrainian Herald*. The clubs are mostly of social nature; however, there is much need for them. They are helping to solve some of the social problems of the "second generation" that does not seem to be able to find its way into American society or does not feel at home there.[29]

The Ukrainian Catholic church officials in America have been working hard since 1933 in creating and maintaining a Catholic youth society. Mr. Bohdan Katamay was the organizer of this movement and edited the monthly journal, *Ukrainian Youth*, for the organization. They also hold annual conventions at which the priests, lay speakers, and the youth take part. There is not much difference between this and the other groups except that the Catholic society stresses the religious aspect.

The youth activity manifests itself first of all in athletics. In the eastern cities they maintain not only basketball and baseball clubs but also competing leagues. In connection with their annual conventions that are held in the summer, they hold track meets, at which the stars from different states compete. The social aspect of their activities are teas, parties, dances, and the presentation of programs for American clubs. The intellectual efforts are revealed in their attempt to publish small papers, that is, the youths themselves financing and running them. In several cities they also have lecturers and discussions, and the girls have classes in embroidery. Such activities keep the young people out of pool halls, saloons, off the streets, and, above all, out of mischief, and give them something better in their place. On the whole, the girls manifest more interest in this movement than the boys. Although the clubs began their group activity only in 1933, they made a good start. In Philadelphia alone they have nine clubs.[30] Probably when this youthful movement reaches its adult stage, it will also mature in thought and assume the responsibility

AVRAMENKO'S FOLK DANCING SCHOOL, CLEVELAND, OHIO

of carrying on the work of the benevolent associations. At least such is both the expressed and the tacit desire of the Ukrainian American parents.

NOTES FOR CHAPTER VI

1. The latest aspect of Russian propaganda is communistic and is financed and directed from Moscow. Efforts are made to convert the Ukrainians in Western Ukraine and the United States to Russian principles. In view of that a daily paper is published in New York for this specific purpose in America.

2. A large book, the *Jubilee Book* (Jersey City, 1936), contains not only the history of the Ukrainian National Association but also many aspects of Ukrainian life in America.

3. "Protocol," supplement to the *Svoboda* (Jersey City), April 6, 1935, pp. 9–12; *Svoboda*, March 16 and April 7, 1937.

4. *Almanac of the Ukrainian Workingmen's Association* (Scranton, 1937), p. 147.

5. *Narodne Slovo* (Pittsburgh), January 28, 1937; *New Life* (Olyphant), July 28, 1932; *America* (Philadelphia), December 24, 1936.

6. Letter from John Masick to the author, February 15, 1935.

7. Letter from Andrew Petach to the author, February 16, 1935.

8. Letter from Peter Smey to the author, February 15, 1935.

9. *Svoboda*, special number, February 21, 1934.

10. *Svoboda*, April 23, 1934.

11. Report of M. Murashko, chairman, at the quadrennial convention in Detroit (*Svoboda*, May 7, 1933).

12. In 1935 the Ukrainian National Association gave sixteen scholarships, varying in amounts from $40 to $150 (*Svoboda*, April 16, 1935).

13. One can hardly see a single issue of a Ukrainian paper in America that does not bring him the terrible happenings in East Galicia—happenings that compare with the worst that ever took place in Africa. The papers of Western Ukraine are censored and therefore cannot print the actual facts. The *Svoboda* for July 24 and 25, 1936, has several examples of this type of unpleasant news. See also *Almanac of the Ukrainian Workingmen's Association* (1928), pp. 129–35.

14. *Svoboda*, May 23, 1933.

15. *Svoboda*, February 12, 1934.

16. Annual report of the secretary of the Obyednania, L. Myshuha (*Svoboda*, November 9, 11, 1935).

17. *Almanac of the Ukrainian Aid Association* (Pittsburgh, 1925), pp. 194–97, 217–27.

18. *Svoboda*, April 22, 1933.

19. Ukrainian Americans contributed $30,000 for the purchase of a building in Lwów to house the invalids of the last war (*Svoboda*, December 1, 1933).

20. Emil Revyuk, *Polish Atrocities in Ukraine* (New York, 1931).

21. *Svoboda*, August 15, 1931; *Narodne Slovo*, May 25, 1933.

22. *Almanac of the Ukrainian Women's League* (New York, 1921–31), pp. 1–18, 52–65.

* The works indicated by an asterisk are in Ukrainian.

23. *Svoboda, March 15, 1932.

24. A brief account of the Ukrainian art exhibits in Boston may be found in the Boston Evening Transcript, July 25, 1930.

25. Yasinchuk, *Za Oceanom, pp. 73–75.

26. *Ukrainian Professionalists in America and Canada (Winnipeg, 1935).

27. Allen H. Eaton, Immigrant Gifts to American Life (New York, 1932), p. 27 et passim.

28. New York Evening Post, April 27, 1931.

29. Louis Adamic, "Thirty Million New Americans," Harper's Monthly Magazine, November, 1934, pp. 684–94.

30. Ukrainian Weekly (Jersey City), July 18, 1936.

CHAPTER VII

THE RELIGIOUS LIFE

INTRODUCTION OF CHRISTIANITY AND GREEK CULTURE INTO THE UKRAINE

ALTHOUGH the Christian religion was widely known in the Ukrainian cities before 988, it was then that Christianity received the official royal recognition as the religion of the land. Because Christianity came there from Greece, it has been often called Greek Catholic. That the new form of religion possessed democratic tendencies is evident from the fact that no efforts were made to force the Greek language into the church services. The usage of the archaic Old Slavic in liturgy was permitted and some of the best Ukrainian pagan religious practices were incorporated.[1]

When the Greek missionaries brought their religious teaching to the Ukraine, they also brought with them architects to construct church edifices and schools, and teachers to train new ministers. Therefore, a measure of Greek culture entered the country with religion. In turn, the Ukrainians became the carriers of Christianity and civilization to the northern Muscovite tribes, the future Russians. According to the requirements of the religion in the Ukraine, the clergymen had to be married before their ordination or to remain single afterward. They were subject to the bishops, who in turn were subject to the patriarch at Constantinople. The religion was colorful and formal, containing ceremonies, images, and pictures.

RELIGIOUS BODIES IN THE UKRAINE

The religious life in the Ukraine has been shaped and modified by the existing political conditions. Since that country was subject to conquests by its neighbors, almost each conqueror attempted to abridge the religious freedom and to force changes. Thus, when Catholic Poland conquered Western Ukraine, after

95

many efforts she eventually forced the Ukrainians, in the closing years of the sixteenth century, to recognize the pope at Rome as their religious head. The Ukrainians, however, were very obstinate and refused to submit themselves to Roman jurisdiction unless the latter agreed not to interfere with their church government, form of worship, and married clergy. Pope Clement VIII made this promise.[2] All the subsequent popes, for the most part, respected this agreement until the present Pius XI. He is endeavoring to invalidate it both in Europe and in America by his efforts to enforce celibacy, such action provoking much opposition among the Ukrainian Americans. A great majority of the Ukrainians, however, have belonged to the church their ancestors handed down to them; it became known as Orthodox.

Following the religious revival movement in northern Europe, historically known as the Reformation, Protestantism took root in Poland and the Ukraine. Many of the higher classes and the gentry became converted to it; but the new religious movement must not have been deeply rooted, for it did not continue far into the seventeenth century. The government as well as the high church officials succeeded in discouraging or suppressing it. At a later date it was reintroduced into the Ukraine by the German settlers. In the second half of the nineteenth century the Ukrainian masses readily accepted the Bible and Protestantism. They withstood the persecution, and before the World War there must have been about two million converts who were loosely organized into groups. A few of their leaders and many thousands of their followers suffered exile to Siberia for their religious activities. Timotey A. Zaitz was the most prominent leader to be exiled.[3]

PRESENT STATUS OF THE CHURCH IN THE UKRAINE

Since the World War, when the Ukraine was again partitioned by her neighbors (with the consent of France and England but without the consent or vote of the Ukrainian people), both the new overlords—Czechs and Rumanians—and the old ones— Poles and Russians—have been using their power to regulate the religious life in the Ukraine. Polish government spies are

ever present in the Ukrainian churches. The government officials are always ready to discriminate against the Ukrainian
Greek Catholics, Orthodox or Protestants, and to favor the Roman Catholics, but the Ukrainians stand fast by their religious
rights in the face of abuses and persecution. Bolshevik Russians
and their agents, the Jewish officials, have been doing their best
to destroy all the existing forms of religion and substitute in place
of it worship of Lenin, Marx, Stalin, and machines. The most
senseless church regulation has been established by Rumania,
who rules over one million Ukrainians in Bessarabia and Bukovina. The Ukrainian language is permitted in church service,
but the moment any government official enters the church, the
priest must begin at once in Rumanian, though not a member
of the congregation understands it.

CONFUSION OF RELIGIOUS CLASSIFICATION IN AMERICA

A big majority of the Ukrainian immigrants in the United
States came from the western provinces of the country that recognized the pope as its religious head; consequently they have
been known as Catholics (Uniates). But because they still, for the
most part, enjoy the old religious rights, services in Old Slavonic,
and married clergy, they officially call their religion Greek
Catholic. That has caused some confusion in America, and
numerous Americans have classed these people as Greeks. Although often lacking in thorough basic knowledge of Christianity, the immigrants were very religious. Their religion had mys-
tic aspects to the point of superstition. An immigrant took off
his hat while passing in front of the church; he often on such
occasions crossed himself likewise. A church had a deep significance in the life of these people.

ATTENDANCE AT FOREIGN CHURCHES

During the first few years of Ukrainian immigration to America, before the Ukrainian churches were organized, the religious
life of these people reached the point of starvation. Though they
hated to attend services in the buildings of their historical oppressors—the Poles—in many cases their religious need impelled

them to do so. The Poles in several instances had their churches already or were building them when the Ukrainians came to America. Those who attended the Polish churches also paid toward their maintenance, but they did not feel at home in the enemy's place of worship. As soon as their own number increased through immigration, they began to organize their own churches. In Shamokin, Pennsylvania, the Polish priest, Ks. Kalinowski, it was reported, upon learning that the Ukrainians were attempting to organize their own church, one Sunday morning in 1884 denounced them from the pulpit and ordered his people to pray that the attempted project might fail.[4]

OBSTACLES TO THE ORGANIZATION OF UKRAINIAN
CHURCHES IN AMERICA

When the Ukrainians thought that they were able to maintain churches of their own, they brought over to America their own priests. The Shenandoah, Pennsylvania, group took the initiative. It appealed to the Metropolitan, Cardinal Sembratovich, the head of the Ukrainian church in Galicia, to send them a priest. Upon receiving money from America to pay the transportation expenses, he sent them a very able young minister in the person of Rev. John Volansky. Since the young missionary was married and going to America for good, he took his wife with him. When the Irish Catholic church officials in Shenandoah and the Bishop of Philadelphia learned of the arrival of a married Catholic priest, they became alarmed and started trouble for him. They even sent demands to Rome that he be recalled at once. The first Sunday Rev. Fr. Volansky was on American soil the priests of the Philadelphia diocese read in their churches the letter by which their bishop was excommunicating him.[5]

While the Irish clergymen were plotting against Volansky, he was laying a foundation for the Ukrainian church and other institutions in America. He organized churches in Shenandoah, Shamokin, and Olyphant in Pennsylvania; he also traveled to other states to serve the spiritual needs of his people. Besides his religious work he, with the aid of his wife, published a newspaper and organized and coached a dramatic club. He also established and managed several co-operative stores. After three years of hard labor, Volansky was recalled to the Ukraine; his work, however, was carried on by his successors.[6] Though the Metropolitan Sembratovich did not want to antagonize the papacy or American Catholics by sending married priests to America, he could not help himself. He had but few priests that were young and unmarried or were widowers; those that were married wanted to take their wives with them to America. Meanwhile, from America came appeals of the immigrants for ministers. In the end, those clergymen were sent that wanted to go. Even then several families were broken up forever. The Irish bishops continued to meddle in Ukrainian church affairs for many years and cause trouble. Because of that interference, two able priests, Rev. Ivan Ardan and Dr. Alexey Tovt (Toth), left the Catholic church.[7] The former became a journalist, while the latter joined the Russian church and became the most potent factor for many years in proselyting the Ukrainians and establishing Russian churches for them.

PIONEER MISSIONARIES

The first few clergymen that were sent to do missionary work in America were, on the whole, very competent men. Next to Volansky, the most outstanding were: Antin Bonchevsky, the beloved pastor at Ansonia, who was a Christian idealist and a hard worker; Paul Tymkevich, the pastor at Yonkers; Ivan Ardan of Olyphant; and the most-loved Nikolai Stefanovich, pastor of the south side church in Pittsburgh. A majority of the pioneer missionaries overworked themselves and died prematurely. Those who came to America afterward, especially in the decade before the World War, did not include many self-sacrificing idealists. On the contrary, there were among them a few who were full of mischief of one type or another. Like most of the immigrants, moneymaking was their chief objective.

THE ERA OF CHURCH BUILDING

Beginning with 1884, the Ukrainian church-building period extended down to 1933. During those years hundreds of necessary and unnecessary edifices were built. This church-building program and resulting expense of maintenance proved to be the

UKRAINIAN CATHOLIC CHURCH
Oakley Boulevard and Rice Street, Chicago

heaviest social burden borne by the people. An exception may be pointed out in the case of the Protestant groups, whose church buildings are smaller and less ornate. The story of the building of churches by the Ukrainian Americans contains numerous unpleasant incidents. Not infrequently a newly arrived priest, anxious to get rich quickly at the expense of his ignorant parishioners, found his golden opportunity when the church building was under construction. Such a dishonest person embezzled thousands of dollars, then left for some other parish in another state. The poor people knew what had happened but, not knowing the English language or the American law, gave up hope of recovering the church funds. They were religiously hoping that "the Lord would punish such sinners." The last financial scheme of this type was tried in one of the churches of Pittsburgh as late as the World War. When the priest found out that the people were not docile and threatened him with arrest on the ground of embezzlement, though he had become a resident in a distant community, he returned the "borrowed money"— several thousand dollars.[8]

EARLY CHURCH GOVERNMENT

There was no bishop or any head of the Ukrainian Catholic church in America until 1907, though there was a need of one. Each church had more or less a congregational form of government; that is, it owned and maintained its building and through its trustees elected or dismissed a priest. That system did not always work out well. Occasionally a clergyman disregarded the rights of his brother-by-profession and did everything in his power to force the other man out of his position and take his place.[9] Then, too, some unprincipled individuals brought discord among the people and caused a religious split according to the provinces from which the people emigrated; thus, the same people of the same language and religion had one church for those who came from Galicia and another for those from the neighboring province of Ruthenia. Frequently these churches, although unfriendly to each other, have been very close neighbors; the best example is found in Pittsburgh, on the south side, where they are within a few feet of each other, the one on Seventh and Carson, the other across the street in the middle of the block. Since the division occurred after the church building was completed and often paid for, each one of the contesting factions tried to take the church property. Law suits followed and caused additional expense and unpleasant feeling. Such was the situation prior to the arrival of the first bishop, the Right Reverend Stephan Ortinsky.

ARRIVAL OF BISHOP ORTINSKY

When Bishop Ortinsky attempted to put an end to chaos and establish order, some of his clergymen rebelled against him. Several congregations refused to deed their church property to the bishop; they either remained independent and, in due time, became Ukrainian Orthodox or sought the protection of the Russian bishop, thus becoming "Russian." Bishop Ortinsky was a young, large, and domineering person. He possessed great energy and no small measure of ability. In his short life in America (he died in 1916), he had his diocese well organized and the clergymen disciplined. He built a large church in Philadelphia, of which he was the pastor. Several thousand people attended the services. He collected money in different Ukrainian churches of the country with which to purchase eighteen buildings in the vicinity of his church. In these buildings he housed a printing establishment with a newspaper, *America;* an orphan asylum housing over one hundred children; a dormitory for some twenty boys, mostly candidates for the priesthood; a meeting place for a club of some three thousand Ukrainian American citizens; and a headquarters for the benevolent society, the Providence, which he organized. Because of his forceful character and exorbitant financial demands, Bishop Ortinsky was disliked by many of his churches.[10] He antagonized the nationalist group when he tried to make the Ukrainian National Association and its newspaper, the *Svoboda*, into a Catholic organization. When he failed in this plan, he set up a competitive organization and newspaper.[11] Although he lived in America less than ten years, he left signs of hard work.

ARRIVAL OF BISHOPS BOHACHEVSKY AND TAKACH

Following Ortinsky's death, Rev. Peter Poniatyshyn, then pastor at Newark, New Jersey, was the temporary administrator of church affairs. The successors of Ortinsky, however, were not appointed until 1923. They are Bishop Konstantin Bohachevsky, for the Ukrainian Catholics from Galicia, and Bishop Wasyl Takach, for the people from Ruthenia. When the two new bishops came over, they endeavored with much zeal and little tact to carry out the instructions of Pius XI. They favored celibacy and attempted to set aside the agreement with the papacy of 1595. The tactless conduct of the two men, combined with lack of patriotism, antagonized most of the Ukrainian American press against them.[12] They have both been storm centers, one or the other, ever since they came to America; for a long time a large percentage of both the clergy and the people had contempt for these two bishops. In 1927 several Ukrainian churches and their priests that were subject to them broke away from Rome and established the Ukrainian Orthodox church of America. Because the church property of these factions that broke away from Rome had at one time been deeded to the bishop, they wanted to regain it through the courts. In a majority of cases the people were victorious over Bishop Bohachevsky, but the victory was very costly. As late as March 15, 1937, the case of one parish in Woonsocket, Rhode Island, was before the state supreme court.[13]

RUSSIAN RELIGIOUS ACTIVITIES

Another aspect of the stormy church life of Ukrainian Americans was the part played by the late Czar Nicholas II, through the Holy Synod of the Russian Orthodox church. Russian Pan-Slavic policy was not confined to the Balkans and Constantinople; it aimed also at the Ukrainian people who were subject to Austria-Hungary until 1918. Russian propaganda in Galicia and Ruthenia dates from 1848. The Czarist regime sent to America hundreds of agents, or recruited them here, for the purpose of proselyting the Ukrainian people, i.e., trying on American soil to convert them to the Russian Orthodox religion and make Russians of them. To this end the government spent $77,850 annually.[14] This Russian money brought a measure of success to its giver as long as the old regime lasted. Through the subsidy of Russia, scores of churches were built, mostly in Pennsylvania, although there is one in Minneapolis and one in Wilton, North

Dakota. Such churches were called "Russian Orthodox," and the people that attended them "Russian." According to Dr. Jerome Davis, a student of Russian immigration, a majority of the one hundred and sixty-nine Russian churches in America (in 1921) were Ukrainian. So few people were recruited in several cases that these "Russian" churches now remain empty, a symbol of one-time Russian policy.

FINANCIAL PRACTICES IN UKRAINIAN CHURCHES

The church-membership fee in the Ukrainian churches, on the whole, is much smaller than in American churches. However, it takes money to maintain church buildings, parish houses (furnished), in many cases church schools that teach Ukrainian, and to pay the officials. Almost always the membership dues have to be collected at the homes of the parishioners by church trustees, priests, or both. A good many Catholic churches have recently established the practice of having the church schools taught by the nuns; formerly this work was done by the choir leaders (*diaks*).[15] In the Orthodox churches not infrequently the clergymen also teach school and direct the choir, i.e., do the work of two or three and receive the pay of one. Such has been the situation during the last few years of financial hardship. The Catholic communicants are also called upon to support the philanthropic organizations. The institutions that solicit such aid are the orphanage in Philadelphia, the convents at Fox Chase and Factoryville in Pennsylvania, and a small theological school for boys at Stamford, Connecticut. Although the chief financial burden of maintaining these institutions falls on the Ukrainian Catholic masses and prosperous individuals, some help also comes in the form of annual gifts from the Ukrainian National Association, American friends, and the Knights of Columbus.[16] The industrial depression, which followed the World War, reduced the annual aid of these institutions, but they are still able to continue with their work.

NUMBER OF CHURCHES MAINTAINED

According to a close investigation based on both the latest church publications and authoritative letters from church officials, in 1936 there were 553 churches, built and maintained by Ukrainians. They were divided into the following sects: Two

Ukrainian Orthodox Church, Wilton. Built in 1916

Ukrainian Catholic Church, Wilton. Built in 1907

RURAL UKRAINIAN CHURCHES IN NORTH DAKOTA

factions were Catholics, one headed by Bishop Bohachevsky, with 118 churches and 88 priests, and the other by Bishop Takach, with 158 churches. The Ukrainian Orthodox also had two factions, one headed by Theodorivich, with 27 buildings, the other by Bishop Bohdan, with 38. The Protestant groups, which are smaller in number, with only 18 churches, are split the most into several sects, the Baptist and Presbyterian being the most numerous.[17] Those that have the label of "Russian" numbered 194 (in 1934) and have a bishop of Ukrainian nationality, Bishop Adam (Filipovsky).[18]

INFLUENCE OF CHURCH AND CLERGY

Clergymen played a prominent part, for better or worse, among the immigrants. They helped to organize many societies and were looked up to by the people, not only for spiritual instruction but also for social leadership. Whenever there was in any parish an able, honest, ideal, hard-working priest, the people highly esteemed him. There were a few clergymen who rose above the rest of their fellow-workers. They found time to do good. Some of them besides carrying on their religious work edited papers, while others studied immigration, wrote articles for the papers and almanacs, or wrote pamphlets. To this group belonged Hrushka, Ardan, Bonchevsky, Dmytriv, and Makar. Those that are now writing include Kinash, Sembratovich, Prystay, and Zabawa in the Catholic church, and the most active of all the present clergymen, Stepan Museychuk, the poet, and K. Kyrstiuk in the Ukrainian Orthodox church. Zygmunt Bychinsky alone represented the Protestant group with his literary contributions.

About 96 per cent of all the Ukrainian clergymen are immigrants, nearly all of whom acquired their education in Europe. The exceptions to this are several Protestant preachers who, though born in the Ukraine, attained their higher education in America. The Catholic clergymen, as a class, are highly educated; they completed Gymnasium and a four-year course in theology in Europe. Three of their priests have a title of Doctor of Philosophy. The Ukrainian Orthodox clergy have in their ranks a rather small number with higher educations, but several are competent and productive workers. In the Russian mission the clergymen are, in the majority of cases, without any higher education or distinctive ability. Most of those of the latter group have had probably the equivalent of six grades of an American public school. Their theological course was likewise very abbreviated, consisting of two to six months of private study. In 1914, when Russian armies entered East Galicia, the agents of that government in America used every means possible to make Russian Orthodox out of Ukrainian immigrants. Almost to the end of the World War, any Ukrainian in America with any kind of intelligence and ability to read and write could have become a Russian priest, if he had wanted to.

The church as an institution has played an important part in the life of the Ukrainian immigrants and their descendants. Besides serving the spiritual need of the people, it has been a social and cultural center. It was in the church halls that the parish libraries were first established. These libraries, meager as they have been, have served as an elevating factor to the people who preferred to go there instead of going to a saloon. In these halls, also, concerts and amateur plays have often been presented, such plays and presentations taking place at the end of the week, mostly on Sunday evenings. The church groups, also, have picnics in the summer out in the country. Large churches have maintained choruses, orchestras, and bands. Likewise during many years the mutual aid associations have had close contact with the church; the same people have belonged to both of them. The clergymen in many cases have helped to organize local lodges and occasionally even have held the head offices in the national organizations. Until recent years, when some local lodges acquired buildings of their own, a'most all their meetings took place in church halls. It is apparent that the church was an inevitable institution, and, until the World War, practically every Ukrainian belonged to one. On Sundays the church buildings were full, and on holidays they were crowded beyond capacity.

DECLINE IN CHURCH ATTENDANCE

During the World War and the years that followed, church attendance among the Ukrainian Americans sustained a setback. The war itself and many evils connected with it brought the people together in small groups for discussion. The fact that the

Christians of one country fought those of another did not appeal to thoughtful people. Then, too, they did not like the idea that the church heads blessed the armies of their countries and wished them much success in killing the enemy. In addition to these causes, the critical attitude of some newspapers toward the acts of the clergy had its effect in lessening interest in religion. Both written and oral antireligious propaganda invaded Ukrainian society in America. It was at first the socialist groups, then the communist agitators, who used to station themselves on Sundays near the church buildings and, the moment the people left the churches, give them propaganda leaflets or invitations to a "lecture." The attempted efforts of the Catholic church authorities to take away some religious rights from the Ukrainians did not do the church cause any good. Consequently church attendance has suffered.[19] The priests are not getting younger either; their youth and vitality are a thing of the past. They are unable to move around swiftly to see their people. A few have been coming to America to take the places of those forty-two Greek Catholic priests who have died, but they do not fit so well into American society.[20] They do not know English or understand the youth born and educated in America. Whether the Ukrainian churches in America will continue as separate units for many decades, the way the Swedish and the German have been able to do, will depend altogether upon the new generations. The future of these churches is not very bright; the reason may be seen from a statement of one of the hard-working priests who has a large family. He wrote in 1936: "I have four sons but not a one of them wants to hear about entering the ministry."[21] Most of the other young men feel the same way.

FUTURE ASPECTS

There are three possibilities for them in the future in America. The Ukrainians may continue to maintain the churches and institutions that they inherited from their ancestors, if they have able leaders; they may join those American churches whose form of religion closely resembles the Ukrainian; or they may go astray. All three of these factors are in evidence already; there are several communities where such situations exist. Americans of the old stock are in a position to help these new Americans to adjust themselves and solve their problems. Much will depend upon the type of welcome the Ukrainians get in American church and society.

NOTES FOR CHAPTER VII

1. Michael Hrushevsky, *Z Istorii Religiynoi Dumki na Ukraini* ("From the History of Religious Thought in Ukraine") (Lwów, 1925), pp. 13–40.

2. Hrushevsky, *Istoria Ukrainy—Rusy* ("History of the Ukraine—Ruthenia") (Lwów, 1905), V, 508–618.

3. "Ukrainian Colonies in North Dakota," *Almanac of Ukrainian Workingmen's Association* (Scranton, 1936), pp. 134–38.

4. "History of the Ukrainian Catholic Parish in Shamokin, Pa.," *Almanac of the Orphan's Home* (Philadelphia, 1935), p. 82; A. Drozdiak, "Pochatok Shamokinskoi hromadi," MS in the possession of the author.

5. Dr. Vladimir Simenovich, "Ukrainian Immigration in the United States," the *Ukraina*, March 13, 1931. Dr. Simenovich came to America in 1887 and was Rev. Fr. Volansky's assistant for a while in social work. He was one of the first immigrants and participated in civic projects until his death in Chicago, in July, 1932.

6. *Ibid.*

7. For particulars about the reception of Dr. Tovt (Toth) by Bishop Ireland of St. Paul, Minnesota, see *Russkey Pravoslavney Calendar* (Pittsburgh, 1934), pp. 102–06; W. P. Shiver, *Immigrant Forces* (New York, 1913), pp. 175–76, 180–81.

8. In describing the conditions among the Ukrainian Americans after the World War, Rev. Alex Prystay has several concrete, unimpeachable facts of financial malfeasance by a few clergymen ("Memoirs of Rev. Alex Prystay" [MSS], pp. 76–79).

9. The story of the Ukrainian Greek Catholic Church of Saint Peter and Paul, Jersey City, is an example of the situation in many other cities. For particulars see *Almanac of the Providence Association* (Philadelphia, 1932), pp. 87–100.

10. Archibald McClure, *Leadership of New America* (New York, 1916), pp. 84–110.

11. "History of the Ukrainian National Association," *Svoboda* (Jersey City), February 21, 1934.

12. The outstanding critic of Bishop Bohachevsky for several years was the *Svoboda* daily, while the most bitter opponent of Bishop Takach has been an influential weekly, the *Amerikansky Russky Viestnik* of Homestead, Pennsylvania. In 1932 about 150 churches subject to the jurisdiction of Bishop Takach protested against his violation of the historic rights of their church (*Ukrainian Herald* [Butler, Pa.], July, 1932).

13. *The Ukrainian Orthodox Church of America* (New York, 1931); "Causes of Disruption of the Ukrainian Greek Catholic Church in the United States," Prystay, *op. cit.*, p. 638; *Dnipro* (Philadelphia), March 15, 1937.

14. Jerome Davis, *The Russian Immigrant* (New York, 1922), p. 91; "Religious Bodies," *United States Department of Commerce Bureau of the Census* (Washington, 1929), II, 514.

* The works indicated by an asterisk are in Ukrainian.

15. The annual expenditures of the Ukrainian churches in Pittsburgh, in 1925, were reported to be $1,629,670. (*ibid.*, p. 1264).

16. *Almanac of the Orphan's Home* (Philadelphia, 1932), pp. 31–53; *Svoboda* (Jersey City), April 16, 1935.

17. These figures do not quite agree with the conclusion of Y. Chyz, who gives 583 as the number of churches; his estimate, however, is based upon data of 1926 (*Almanac of the Ukrainian Workingmen's Association* [Scranton, 1936], p. 122). The Presbyterian group, though one of the smallest, has played a more important part in educating Ukrainian immigrants within its reach than any other similar group. In 1932 there were only five of these churches in America, but during the thirty years of their history they were instrumental in giving higher education to about sixty young people (letter from Rev. Basil Kusiv to the author, March 23, 1932). Rev. O. Mycyk furnished the information in regard to the number of churches in Archbishop Theodorovich's diocese, October 6, 1936.

18. These so-called Russian figures were computed partly on personal investigation and based partly on the study of these churches in the *Russkey Pravoslavney Calendar* (Pittsburgh, 1934), pp. 149–63.

19. In some towns the church attendance fell off 50 per cent (Ivan Chienko, "Aspects of the Ukrainian Religious Life in America," *Narodna Vola* [Scranton], November 26, 1921).

20. *Almanac of the Orphan's Home* (Philadelphia, 1935), p. 157.

21. Letter from Rev. Joseph Zelechivsky to the author, May 19, 1936.

CHAPTER VIII

THE PRESS

THE Ukrainian press in the United States has had a stormy history. There were any number of individuals ready to start newspapers but there was not so ready a public to support every paper founded.[1] Probably not many of the publications merited popular support. In the end, the only newspapers whose financial side was taken care of were those that represented the benevolent associations; these were the papers that weathered the early hardships and survived.

THE BEGINNING OF THE UKRAINIAN PRESS IN AMERICA

On March 1, 1868, a Ukrainian political exile, Agapius Honcharenko, a resident of San Francisco, started the first Russian newspaper in America. He was not only its founder but its owner, editor, and printer as well.[2] He named this paper the *Alaska Herald and Svoboda*. One-half of the publication was in English, the other in Russian; occasionally he printed articles in his native tongue, Ukrainian.[3] It was not, however, until August 15, 1886, that the first Ukrainian paper was started in the United States. In that year the missionary, John Volansky, started a semimonthly, *America*, in Shenandoah, Pennsylvania. Volansky and his wife at first did all the work that was involved in its publication. The next year two educated immigrants came to Volansky's assistance; Vladimir Simenovich became an editor and Wasyl Sarich a typesetter. The *America* was enlarged, and the annual subscription set at two dollars. After Volansky's recall to Europe, the paper with all its equipment became the property of the Ukrainian church in Shenandoah, but his successor, Rev. Fr. Andruchovich, so mismanaged the project that in less than a year (in 1890) the publication was suspended.[4] In 1891 Andruchovich started a weekly, *Ruske Slovo*, in Shenandoah,

111

and Rev. Fr. Hrushka began the publication of *Novey Svit* in Jersey City. Neither of these papers lasted long, both disappearing in the same year.[5]

CHARACTER OF THE PRESS

The entire history of the Ukrainian press in the United States covers only fifty years. During that time (1886–1936) seventy-nine different newspapers were established, a large percentage of which exist no longer.[6] A majority of the papers were in the Ukrainian language or dialect, some partly in Russian, and still others, in recent years, in English. More than half of the publications were weeklies; others were semimonthlies and monthlies. A large percentage of illiteracy among the early immigrants was the chief reason for the instability of their press. Neither is it justifiable to suppose that "the fittest" papers survived, for there were some of better quality that perished. At the same time several publications, especially those that were labeled as "humorous," did not deserve public support and did not get it, for their editors neither possessed nor practiced the art of humor, indulging instead in personalities. Such periodicals ordinarily lasted but a few months each. Several religious publications likewise were started but did not survive many years; after intervals, new ones took their places.

THE EDITORS

During the first twenty years of the history of the Ukrainian press in America the clergymen, in most cases, were the editors, the most noted of whom were Hryhorey Hrushka, Nestor Dmytriv, Stephan Makar, and Antin Bonchevsky. The decades that followed saw a doctor, lawyers, teachers, students, and adventurers serving in editorial capacities. Among that group the clergymen and the lawyers, all with European education, predominated. Rarely was there a trained professional journalist holding such a position. This situation partly re-enacted that period of American history when a person tried any profession to which he, at a given time, felt a calling. Thus this "calling" rather than educational qualifications had to serve as a prerequisite, and in consequence, as may be expected, the professional standard was not high. Thus far the Ukrainian Americans have not produced a great journalist. Nearly all their present newspapermen were born and educated abroad.

DUTIES OF THE EDITORS

An editor is a big man in the opinion of his immigrant readers. The editorial task, however, has not been rosy, for besides editing the paper and often almanacs likewise, an editor also had to deliver frequent public addresses. During the early years of the Ukrainian press in America some of the papers also published popular booklets, which were sold in the small bookstore that nearly every paper maintained.[7] The positions of the editors of the papers that are published by the benevolent associations, as well as those of their associates, are filled, as a rule, by elections at the quadrennial conventions. Although some of the organizations pay these officials as high as two hundred and fifty dollars a month, there is little competition for the offices; rarely are there as many as a half-dozen candidates. Several men served in journalistic work for many years; those serving the longest include Ivan Ardan (retired), Joseph Stetkevich, Emil Revyuk, Vladimir B. Lototzky, Antin Curkovsky (retired), Luke Myshuha, Yaroslav Chyz, Matthew Chandoha, and Stephen Varzaly.

INFLUENCE OF THE PRESS

The Ukrainian press in America, which soon became national in circulation rather than local, had an important duty to perform, its chief task being to educate its readers and listeners. Yes, listeners—those people who themselves were unable to read but who listened to others read their papers aloud. In due course of time a considerable percentage of the adult illiterate immigrants learned to read in their native tongue in America. The immigrant press for many years had to reach the people who were unable to avail themselves of papers in English. Because of their European background, the editors devoted much of their attention to the news from Europe in general and from the Ukraine in particular; they also informed their readers about America as they themselves understood it. Most of the Ukrainian papers lived up to the great objective of educating their readers,[8] although, unfortunately, there have been some which did much the opposite. Like the church, the press was a great factor in creating and maintaining public opinion. Since

UKRAINIAN NEWSPAPERS IN THE UNITED STATES

the World War it has become more influential than the former organization, for it reaches more people oftener. At first the two institutions co-operated; then they passed through a period of antagonism and finally assumed the present position of aloofness toward each other.

It is interesting to note in this connection that until 1905 even the Ukrainian nationalist leaders called their churches and papers in America "Little Russian."[9] Owing to the long foreign domination of their country and the prohibition of their native schools, racial consciousness was mostly dormant among the Ukrainian masses. After that date, for about fifteen years, they, as a rule, named their institutions "Ruthenian," but since then the name "Ukrainian" has been gaining ground. Such was the development of Ukrainian nationalism in America; it favorably compared with a similar movement in Europe. At the same time Americanization was going on gradually among these people, and their press began to contain articles and editorials on American topics as well as European.

EVIDENCES OF FACTIONALISM

Just as the organizations of Ukrainian Americans are divided into pro-Russian and Ukrainian nationalist factions, so is their press. As a matter of fact, the press played its part in splitting these people, although the root of factional feeling goes back to Europe. From the time such factional papers were established to this day they have maintained an antagonistic attitude. The readers, of course, taking their cue from the leaders, acted accordingly when they met their fellow-countrymen in daily life. Since the World War Ukrainian nationalism has been able to gain ground over Russian-Imperialistic and communistic propaganda, among these people. Besides the two chief factions, there are smaller groups within each of them that differ with one another. To express their differences they often establish newspapers, and at times the party feeling is very bitter, as revealed on the pages of their organs.

PUBLICATIONS OF THE PRO-RUSSIAN FACTION

In 1936 the pro-Russian faction among the Ukrainian Americans published eight papers. These were printed either in literary Ukrainian or in a dialect, in a mixture of Ukrainian and Russian, in Russian, or in English. The oldest, largest, and most influential among them is *Amerikansky Russky Viestnik*, or, shortened, *Viestnik* ("Herald"), of Homestead, Pennsylvania. It is published weekly in Ukrainian mountaineer dialect and is the official organ of a benevolent association. This paper also publishes two supplements, *Sokol Sojedinenija* and *Svit Ditej* ("Child's World"), for the young people. Other benevolent associations publish a semiweekly, *Pravda* ("Truth"), in Philadelphia; a weekly, *Prosvita* ("Enlightenment"), at McKeesport; and a weekly, *Svit* ("World"), at Wilkes-Barre. A small group in New York is publishing *Lemko*. In New York City also the communists publish a daily paper in Ukrainian, the *Ukrainian Daily News*. All these papers are published by and for the Ukrainians, though most of them serve as agencies for the advancement of the Russian empire.[10]

THE UKRAINIAN NATIONALIST PRESS

The Ukrainian nationalist press in America has advocated the independence of the Ukraine. Its most important branch is the press that is owned by the benevolent associations. At the head of the list is the largest paper, the *Svoboda* ("Liberty") daily, of Jersey City. Its circulation is about fourteen thousand, reaching the members of the Ukrainian National Association throughout the country, for whom it is published, and the subscribers on the American continents, as well as those in Europe and in Asia. Other leading papers of this group are the two triweeklies, *America* (Philadelphia) and *Narodna Vola* ("People's Will") (Scranton), and a weekly, *Narodne Slovo* ("National Word"), which is published in Pittsburgh. Several other weeklies are published by independent smaller groups: the *Sitch Call* (Newark), the *Nationalist* (New York), *Nash Stiah* ("Our Banner"), in Chicago, and the *Ukrainian Gazette* (Detroit). The first two are published in Ukrainian and English, the others in Ukrainian. There are four semimonthlies: *Dnipro* (Philadelphia)—the organ of the Ukrainian Autocefalous Orthodox church; *Nove Zhitia* ("New Life") in Olyphant—the organ of the Concord Benevolent Association; *Hromada* (Detroit)—an independent publication; and *Visty z Ohio* ("News from Ohio") published in Cleveland. There are also three monthly magazines in Ukrainian. Two of them are published by churches—the *Ukrainsky Vistnyk* ("Ukrainian Herald") at Carteret, N.J., by the Ukrainian Orthodox church and the *Missionary* at Philadelphia by the Catholic church; the third, *Boyevi Zharty* (New York), is a humorous publication.

Nearly every Ukrainian paper in America has an English section or supplement. The following papers have been appearing in English (for a duration of five months to five years): *Ukrainian Weekly* (Jersey City) and the *Rising Star* (Detroit), which are weeklies; *Ukrainian Youth* (Philadelphia) a Catholic periodical, the *Ukrainian Chronicle* (Philadelphia), the *Trident* (Chicago), and *Ukrainian Youth* (New Britain, Conn.) an Orthodox periodical, which are monthlies. These publications are financed and published by the young people.

Altogether the Ukrainian Americans are supporting twenty-nine papers. It is really a small number in proportion to the Ukrainian population and in view of the fact that several smaller papers actually have only a few hundred readers.

The oldest existing papers are the *Viestnik* and the *Svoboda;* they date their origin back to 1892 and 1893, respectively. Before they finally became established in their present homes, each of them—as well as some other papers—migrated from one town to another with the change of residence of the editor, often a priest. Thus the *Svoboda* was moved from Jersey City to Shamokin, Mount Carmel, Olyphant, Scranton, New York, and again to Jersey City. The *Viestnik* was published in Mahonoy City and Scranton, Pennsylvania, New York City, and its present place, Homestead, Pennsylvania. During the second and third decades of the twentieth century, the papers did not have to move much.

It is apparent that the Ukrainian press in America faced obstacles and had to conquer them or be vanquished itself. In the first place, it was hard to buy Ukrainian type faces, the Latin alphabet not being used. Then also, not being a member of any large news-getting syndicate, it could not avail itself of rapid service. This difficulty, however, was negligible, owing to the fact that the immigrant papers were weeklies and had ample opportunity to gather news from the American press. But, in publishing these weeklies, for many years one man only—the editor—was held responsible for all the articles.[11] Since the World War some newspapers have paid correspondents in Europe; none has as yet paid reporters in American cities, although they print frequent reports of Ukrainian social activity over a wide area. The outstanding obstacle these papers had to overcome was financial. The advertising, which is the chief source of income of the American press, does not figure prominently in the immigrant papers, and the Ukrainian press is no exception. To be sure, there are a few advertisements, but they are small and do not appear regularly. The financial burden, therefore, has had to rest upon the subscribers and readers. The only papers that have had steady readers were those that have been published by the organizations. All others found it difficult to maintain themselves and sooner or later had to be discontinued.

CONTENTS OF THE PAPERS

Not having a paying advertising section, the Ukrainian papers are small in dimension. Most of them contain only four pages. The first page is devoted to the news of the world and the United States, obtained mostly from the American papers, the radio, and the Ukrainian papers that are brought from Europe. The influence of the American newspapers upon some of the papers is apparent, especially in the way crime is publicized on the front page. If the American source of supply of crime news is inadequate, that from Europe helps fill up the space. The second page contains an editorial, articles by social contributors from various cities, and reprints of some easy Ukrainian story. The second and third pages in some papers have frequent reports of the trials of Ukrainian political prisoners in Galicia by the Polish courts, such reports being reprints from Ukrainian papers published abroad and lasting for weeks at a time. The third page may also contain discussions of current events. The last page, as a rule, contains advertisements, club announcements, and articles on Americanization that have been supplied by the Foreign Language Information Service.

PRESS RIVALRY

An ordinary Ukrainian newspaper reader is like the old American village resident or retired farmer; he is thorough and reads every line. Therefore it is important, or should be, what the papers print. A careful observation of hundreds of immigrants of various nationalities reveals that they read the editorial more carefully than an average American reader. Considering the amount of work of the Ukrainian editors, their editorials, on the whole, have been well prepared. Unfortunately, occasionally they have spoiled their records by editorials against a rival paper or a rival editor; this has been one of the most unwholesome experiences confronting the readers. There was a time when some of the readers also, under the influence of their papers, took sides with their editors and wrote uncomplimentary things about a rival paper. In recent years, however, the readers have adopted an attitude of aloofness, though the editors still continue their polemics at intervals. Thus the combinations of rival papers such as the *Svoboda* and *Narodna Vola*, *Prosvita* and *Amerikansky Russky Viestnik*, as well as others, frequently maintain a hostile attitude toward each other. Then, again, the only communistic paper, the *Ukrainian Daily News*, often takes issue with some other Ukrainian paper. Most likely, as long as the immigrant intellectuals continue to edit these newspapers, they will adhere to their old habits. With the advent of the American-born in publishing Ukrainian papers, one could expect a change for the better.

POETIC CONTRIBUTIONS

An interesting feature of the Ukrainian press in America is the frequent appearance of poems. There is hardly an issue without a verse, and on the occasion of the national or religious holidays a number of poems or verses are received by the press. Though most of the readers are people of little education, several of them possess poetic inclinations and write for their favorite newspapers. In the post-war period the number of such contributors vastly increased with the arrival of an intelligent immigrant element. The sum total of the poetic contributions for any one year is quite large, although not much of it is of any literary value. Thus far, the only poems that appeared with regularity that probably will eventually count as permanent literature have been those of Musey Stepanchuk, a paraphrase of the name of Stepan Musey-chuk, a Ukrainian Orthodox priest now of Youngstown, Ohio. His poems deal with various topics and appear in several poetic forms. He has had his poems printed in the *Svoboda* daily for several years; if collected, his writings would make a handsome volume.[12] But because his work has not appeared in book form, the competent literary critics have not passed judgment on it. In Canada a few young Ukrainian poets of Museychuk's caliber have received favorable criticism from their own and Canadian critics. The Canadian Ukrainians, though smaller numerically, have produced more literary talent than their brethren south of the border line.

FUTURE OF THE FOREIGN PRESS IN AMERICA

The prospect for the future of the Ukrainian press in the United States is not bright. As a matter of fact, it is dark, and its end may not be far off. Ever since the American government closed its doors to southeastern European immigration, it more or less signaled a death warning to the press of these peoples in America. When one considers the rapidity with which many Ukrainians have been Americanized, it is not hard to see that, with the passing of the immigrant generation, the papers it has established will also pass out. The second generation cannot remain Ukrainian; it is a part of America. According to one of the poets, the Ukrainians in America are like a big cake of ice that is surrounded by a moving warm current, bound to melt and become a part of the current itself. The Jews alone of many peoples have been able to live in various countries for centuries and preserve their nationality and religion with success. The other races under similar conditions became assimilated; the only marks or living monuments are their names, which bespeak racial origin. However, as it is seen from the newspaper reports in our large cities at the time of naturalization hearings, a considerable number of immigrants are Americanizing their names; to this act they are frequently encouraged by the Americans themselves—thus Bodinski becomes "Boden," Rugiero, "Rogers," Rubenstein, "Rubens," Belenko, "Belen," etc.

AMERICAN PAPERS IN UKRAINIAN HOMES

Besides reading their own papers and the Russian, a large number of Ukrainians read American dailies.[13] They read their native press for the news from Europe and the Ukraine, the American papers for the world-news, the local news, the sports page, and the comic section. Sunday papers are read more widely than the dailies by both the immigrants and their children. Realizing the value of gaining thousands of new readers, some of the papers in Cleveland, Ohio, have regular reporters of various nationalities in their city and occasionally send a reporter to European countries who writes from there stories that would interest the foreign-born readers. The American-born people, though in many cases able to read Ukrainian, naturally turn to American papers, for it is easier for most of them to read English than the language of their parents. The older generation was not altogether uncognizant of the problems of the youth, and some steps have already been taken to have the Ukrainian papers in English, that is, papers published in English that cover many Ukrainian subjects.

THE TRANSITION FROM UKRAINIAN TO ENGLISH

The transition period from the purely Ukrainian papers to Ukrainian-English or English was about 1930, although even prior to that time some efforts were made. The Ukrainian National Association and its paper the *Svoboda* led the way in 1925.[14] At first it published a *Juvenile Magazine*, but in 1932 it discontinued this monthly and began to publish the *Ukrainian Weekly* in its place as a supplement to the *Svoboda* daily. When the first issues of the *Ukrainian Weekly* appeared, they received severe condemnation from the critics in the Ukraine, who looked upon the project as a willing effort at abandoning the Ukrainian language, a sign of weakness on the part of the Ukrainian Americans. The critics revealed more native patriotism than consideration of

American conditions. A few Ukrainians in America protested also that "we should teach the youth the Ukrainian language rather than give it up," but their protests were of short duration. Scores of communities have Ukrainian population that is not large enough to maintain private schools; then, of course, there are thousands of individual families scattered widely over the continent who have no opportunity or ambition to educate their children in Ukrainian. The newspaper in English became an instant success, for it was well received by the Ukrainian youth and became a means of contact among the young people scattered throughout the country. Its financial side is taken care of by the reader's membership in the junior division of the Ukrainian National Association. Its editor, Stephen Shumeyko, LL.B., is American-born but knows the Ukrainian language and translates and interprets Ukrainian history as well as the best of literature to those whose parents wish them to know more valuable things about the Ukraine. Once the ice was broken, it was easy to sail. It was not long after the *Ukrainian Weekly* became established that nearly all other papers began to publish either an English page at least once a week or separate English publications intended for the youthful readers, who either do not read Ukrainian at all or read it with difficulty. The Catholic church publishes the only monthly of this type, *Ukrainian Youth*, through which it attempts to inculcate religious teaching and Ukrainianism in its readers.

Several independent periodicals that were tried in English did not last long; as a rule, they terminated their existence within a few months. Those that are now published by the benevolent organizations or churches should be able to carry on because a larger number of people support them financially. The immigrants are willing to spend their money for these publications in English, provided they will educate the youth to the realization of the value of the benevolent associations, churches, and other institutions, so that, when they themselves yield to the inevitable, their children may carry on the work started by them. A small number of university graduates in journalism and art found employment with American papers. When the number of those so educated increases, probably a few of them will some day undertake the publication of the papers that are now published in Ukrainian and carry them on as long·as there is a demand for them, eventually publishing them in English.

NOTES FOR CHAPTER VIII

1. Miroslav Sichinsky, prominent Ukrainian immigrant, worked with four Ukrainian newspapers—*Svoboda, Robitnyk, Narod,* and *Ukrainska Gazeta*—within the space of about five years. The last three of the mentioned papers were established and disappeared within the experience of Sichinsky (Robert E. Park, *The Immigrant Press and Its Control* [New York and London, 1922], pp. 333–36).

2. A more complete account may be found in Honcharenko's memoirs, **Spominki Ahapia Honcharenka* (Kolomea, 1894), pp. 31–34.

3. In 1872, Honcharenko's health failing him, he sold his English section of the paper but desired to continue the *Svoboda* in Russian. The issue of September 1 (p. 4), which the author has, contains a brief discourse in Ukrainian. Since his health did not improve, he was forced to discontinue his journalistic work and moved onto his farm near Hayward, California.

4. Julian Batchinsky, **Ukrainska Immigracia* (Lwòw, 1914), pp. 286–87.

5. *Ibid.,* p. 445.

6. The following Ukrainian papers are no longer published: *Amerika* (of Shenandoah, Pa.), *Ruske Slovo, Novey Svit, Cerkovna Nauka, Osa, Pastyr, Zirnycia, Robotnik, Postup, Molot, Nasha Zizn, Amerikansky Holos, Sojuz, Zazula, Chlopsky Paragraph, Haydamaky, Meta, Dushpastyr, Shershen, Rusin, Amerikanskaya Rus, Zaoceanska Rus, Diakouchitel, Zirka, Lubov, Trud, Nauka, Hirnyk, Batih, Prolom, Iskra, Ukrainska Gazeta, Robitnyk, Ukraina, Tochilo, Bazar, Seech, Dzvin, Narod, Ukrainsky Vistnyk* (Detroit), *Ukrainska Besida, Catolycky Provid, Holos Mazepinciv, Nova Ukraina, Nova Hromada, Niva, Prosvita, Nestorian, Juvenile Magazine,* the *Ukrainian Review, Zinochy Svit,* and the *Trident* (Pittsburgh). Some of these papers are listed in Batchinsky's book (*op. cit.,* pp. 443–61).

7. Several immigrant authors had their stories, poems, and plays printed in the newspapers; and, whenever there was sufficient demand for one of them, it appeared in separate book form. Thus the following writings of Julian Chupka (Buzko) appeared in the *Svoboda* paper in 1893: "Pictures of America," "Constitution of the United States of North America," and "Something about the Laws and Courts of the United States, Especially in Pennsylvania." Nestor Dmitriv wrote articles in the same paper on the subject of Ukrainian immigration. Stephan Makar had several of his stories and plays printed in the *Svoboda;* the same newspaper also printed M. Kostyshyn's poems and Sava Charnecky's poems and stories, as well as the stories of Zigmunt Bychinsky, Michael Byela, and others. The *Sojuz,* Presbyterian paper of Pittsburgh, although it lived only about ten years (1908–18), was responsible for the publication of a number of religious books in Ukrainian.

8. Lev Yasinchuk, *Za Oceanom* (Lwòw, 1930), pp. 75–83.

9. **Svoboda* (Jersey City), October 15, 1893.

* The works indicated by asterisks are in Ukrainian.

10. According to Andrew Dubovoy, who is well informed on the subject of Russian immigration, it is the Ukrainian intellectuals who publish such Russian papers in the United States as *Rassvet, Russky Fashist, Novoye Russkoye Slovo, Russia,* and others (letter from Andrew Dubovoy to the author, March 7, 1935).

11. The Ukrainian American press reprints with regularity news items and articles from the Ukrainian papers that are brought from abroad. Therefore, the remark of one of the editors in Pennsylvania to the author (in 1932) was not an idle joke: "I have two pairs of scissors and no available articles to cut out." However, almost under no condition do the Ukrainian papers in America reprint good articles from one another.

12. A committee was organized in 1936 in Passaic to raise funds for the publication of Museychuk's writings. Its initial success gives indication that its aims will be fulfilled.

13. Although there are homes with two Ukrainian papers as well as a local American, in contrast to these there is a much larger number of homes without any newspapers.

14. A decision was made by the convention of the Ukrainian National Association, which was held at Rochester, New York, to publish a monthly magazine in English for its 10,000 members (*The Interpreter* [New York], May 1925, p. 15).

CHAPTER IX

SOCIAL ACTIVITIES, MUSICAL ORGANIZATIONS AND CIVIC ENTERPRISES

UNTIL various states passed laws regulating hours and conditions of work, the "new immigrants" who furnished the country with the bulk of its low-priced industrial labor supply, especially in the years before the World War, had little time or energy for recreation, social activity, or night-school work. At that time a twelve-to-fourteen-hour day was not out of the ordinary for the manual laborer, and a long day likewise faced the woman who worked in an industrial establishment. Because of the conditions under which the Ukrainians worked and lived, the home with its roomers and boarders and their friends and acquaintances was for many years the center of social contact and the smallest social unit.

Next to the home, in the days of preprohibition, the saloon served as a neighborhood gathering center, for the workers frequented the saloon more often than they did the church or any other kind of society. Even if they did not spend much in the saloons, a majority of men frequented them. After prohibition went into effect—as much as it did go into effect—the habitual drunkard still found the means by way of dark alleys to buy a drink that often poisoned him; but the rest of the saloon frequenters had to find some other place for social gathering. Therefore prohibition, with all its faults, unquestionably had a good effect upon the Ukrainian Americans.

THE CHURCH AS A SOCIAL CENTER

The church, as previously described, served not only as a place of worship but also as a wholesome social center. Various societies became organized in connection with the churches, having their meetings in the church halls. A considerable number had small parish libraries and reading-rooms,[1] consequently people came to the church building often. Today several larger churches have halls that are being used for gymnasium work and basketball. To keep the people closely connected with these institutions, a few even installed billiard tables. In several cities Boy Scout troops have been maintained in the halls of the Ukrainian churches, and in these same halls women's sewing circles meet. Here also are found the facilities for preparing and serving church dinners.

THE CHURCH SCHOOLS

The church schools, which are held in the afternoon after the dismissal of the public schools, teach reading and writing in Ukrainian and religion. Ukrainian immigrants, who themselves have learned much in America about the country of their birth, desire that their children learn Ukrainian when there is an opportunity.[2] Ordinarily they attend these schools, some irregularly, for a period of two and three years. There is one small full-time Catholic Ukrainian high school in Stamford, Connecticut, established in 1933 by Bishop Bohachevsky for preparing boys for the priesthood. A similar institution was under construction in Chicago in 1935–36 on Rice Street and Oakley Boulevard by the monastic order of St. Basil.

THE DRAMATIC CLUBS

Of much importance have been the church dramatic clubs, which have included in their numbers younger people of more than average intelligence and ambition. These groups have staged amateur Ukrainian plays, which have often drawn large audiences. These performances, which for the most part have been sufficiently easy not to require professional skill or heavy expenditure, have portrayed life in Ukrainian villages. Occasionally, however, when historical productions were attempted, the services of persons with professional training and experience were required, and the performance was staged in a larger auditorium than the church hall. It was then that the immigrants with European operatic and stage experience began to appear before the Ukrainian public in America. But, for the most part, the most appealing plays have been those of comical and musical character.

With the exception of a few, all of that repertoire of plays available for Ukrainian presentation in America, which approaches the neighborhood of one hundred, are imported from Europe.[3] A small number, written by the immigrants themselves, deal with American immigrant life. Since 1920 the tendencies have been to enlist the services of the second generation for dramatic work, and in the large cities a superior type of dramatic talent often reveals itself.

MUSICAL ORGANIZATIONS

Since there was a necessity for musical groups, a number of youth orchestras and several bands have been organized and maintained alongside other organizations. The mixed choirs from the churches have held a very prominent place in Ukrainian social activities in America. Aside from their participation in church worship—singing being the chief attraction of Ukrainian church services[4]—they have often furnished music for various activities. The quality of the singing depends upon the size of the congregation from which the talent is drawn, the ability of the singers themselves, and the skill of the director (*diak*). A *diako-uchitel*, or choir director, is a man who has had some training in music in general but special training in church music. A few of them have been good singers. Several of these directors, at one time or another, have developed fine choirs, which have appeared in numerous concerts before both their own people and the American public. The number of good choir leaders has diminished in recent years, for no new ones are coming from Europe, and the Russian bishops have enticed many of those already in America into the Orthodox priesthood, giving them a few months of special private tutoring in theology. The two Ukrainian Orthodox sects ordained several also through a similar process.[5] As the occasion demanded, either Bishop Ivan Theodorovich or Rev. K. Kyrstiuk offered short theological courses to the candidates before their ordination. Although it is true that most of such specially created priests are more choir leaders than priests and habitually devote much of their attention to the choirs, their other church duties—teaching school and tending to their ministry—take so much of their time that they are not always able to do justice to the singing. Yet three or four of them have succeeded in maintaining good choirs with which they have won local popularity.

Much of the success of the Ukrainian singing groups and individuals is due to their inherited singing gifts, the experience they have had in singing folk songs from their childhood, the quality of the songs themselves, and the characteristics of the language.[6] In the Ukraine there is much singing; in fact, every aspect of Ukrainian life is expressed in song. The Christmas carols alone number hundreds; then there are the songs for the spring and Easter season, a few dating to a pre-Christian Era; harvest songs, love songs, wedding songs, and the most important historical *dumy* only partly complete the list. A boy or girl in the native country who tends the cattle in the summer knows hundreds of them. Several collectors of Ukrainian folk songs have printed thousands of them, but much still remains unwritten and uncollected.[7]

ADOPTION OF UKRAINIAN FOLK SONGS BY THE RUSSIANS

It is often expressed that the spiritual wealth of the Ukraine is primarily its folk songs. Its neighbors and oppressors, after depriving it of political independence and freedom, attempted to steal its culture by stealing even its songs. The chief offenders have been the Russians, in both Europe and America. They have been singing the Ukrainian Christmas carols, "Koliady" and "Schedrivky," and telling the foreign public that they were Russian; they did the same with Ukrainian secular songs, even translating a few of them into English "from Russian." The American public in general has recently acquired a sufficient knowledge of Ukrainian music to detect the Russian theft, and radio announcers frequently require the performers to acknowledge when they are singing Ukrainian songs. In western Europe, on the other hand, the Russians are still able to deceive the general public.[8]

OTHER RECREATION CONNECTED WITH THE CHURCH

Regardless of how many organizations the Ukrainians have in America, the church, even though it is broken into several sects and has a much diminished attendance, still attracts the largest number of people. In order to succeed in their activities, other social groups often solicit the support of the churches. Because of the fact that there are a few religious factions, rivalry exists among them, and they often attempt to outdo one another in religious and civic activities. During the summertime the favorite social function is the picnic. In thickly populated regions "Catholic Day" and "Ukrainian Day" picnics are the vogue; such occasions draw many thousands of people. Even Bishop Bohachevsky has been participating in Catholic picnics in Pennsylvania. The Ukrainian Orthodox churches, political clubs, and the local units of the benevolent associations likewise hold frequent summer outings. In fact, where there are many organizations, hardly a Sunday passes without one. These serve two purposes: the one is obviously recreation; the other, a means of raising funds for some worthy cause. Whenever the Ukrainians attend these gatherings, they forget their worries and truly reveal their social nature.

HOLIDAYS: RELIGIOUS AND NATIONAL

The Ukrainian Americans celebrate several native national as well as religious holidays during the year. Their church holidays fall fourteen days later than American, because they still adhere to the Julian calendar. To many of them the first of November means as much as the Fourth of July to the Americans, for it stands for a similar idea. An equally popular yearly occurrence is Shevchenko Day, which is a birthday celebration of the greatest Ukrainian poet, who next to Christ is dearest to the Ukrainian millions. Franko Day is a similar commemorative celebration to the second noted poet. Other noted writers are kept in memory in a like way. Instead of celebrating on a given day, it is the custom among these people in America to choose any Sunday in the month when the event to be commemorated occurred. The observance consists of a special Sunday service and a mass meeting in the afternoon that lasts for three or four hours. At the latter, the program, as a rule, includes several short talks, a main address, and music, vocal and instrumental.

Family solidarity is evidenced in the way entire families attend these celebrations in groups. Although the second generation speaks better English than Ukrainian, it still knows sufficient of the latter to understand it readily and to use it. The third generation, according to authoritative reports, knows no Ukrainian and is thoroughly American. Yet lectures, plays, and concerts have a way of bringing all three generations together; even if they do not all understand everything, they like to be together.

ATHLETICS

Of late years the participation of the youth in athletics has stimulated the older generation to attend the games. That Ukrainian American youth have mastered most of the American sports may be proved by the part they have played in high-school and college athletics and their membership on the 1932 and 1936 United States Olympic teams.[9] Baseball and basketball games especially have proved attractive among the Ukrainian Americans, principally because their sons often participate in these sports. In 1932 an amateur Ukrainian baseball team of Scranton, Pennsylvania, frequently had an attendance of four thousand or more at an ordinary Sunday-afternoon game with some other amateur team composed of miners or policemen. But, of course, not all the crowd was Ukrainian.

Another sport which has attracted the men on some occasions is the wrestling match, especially when one of the participants has been advertised as a fellow-countryman. Some of these wrestlers in America are Ukrainian and are advertised as such for the nights when they have bouts in towns having a large Ukrainian population; otherwise their Jewish managers advertise them as "Russian," expecting a large American attendance.

INTELLECTUAL INTERESTS

Aside from newspaper reading, not many Ukrainian Americans are exhaustive readers, either for recreation or for study. Therefore, only a few books have been published for them in America. Those that do not read in Ukrainian because of indifference, as a rule do not read much in English either. An average

Ukrainian prefers to take his recreation at the movies, if he has the choice of the two. Out of several types of intellectual entertainment available, however, a Ukrainian rarely turns down a good lecture, especially when given by some able and authoritative person. The ordinary man attends both for pastime and for the purpose of learning; but those who have come under the influence of Bolshevik propaganda attend to see if an opportunity will present itself to argue with the speaker, even if they have neither idea nor knowledge of the subject.

The American night school attracts some individuals in large cities. Much more success could be attained in this type of work among the Ukrainians if the classes in Americanization and citizenship were held in Ukrainian buildings, to which these people habitually go, and taught by Ukrainian Americans. Such classes have been maintained successfully for years by Ukrainian Presbyterian churches in Newark, New Jersey, and in Pittsburgh. In Detroit, in 1935, Ukrainian educators co-operated with the evening-school officials by offering lectures in Ukrainian on historical and scientific subjects. These classes were held in public-school buildings.[10] Some measure of success was attained. The same year, also in evening classes, courses were given in Ukrainian language and literature at Columbia University.[11]

CO-OPERATION WITH AMERICAN GROUPS

Thus far the discussion of this chapter has dealt with social activities confined primarily to Ukrainian environment. But there are several groups that come in contact with American organized life. The first organized Ukrainian participation in American civic enterprise was in 1887, in Shenandoah, Pennsylvania, where the first Ukrainian church in America, under the leadership of Rev. Fr. Volansky, took part in a Fourth of July celebration.[12] Since then, at various times, they have participated in numerous celebrations in many cities. During the World War they supported patriotic activities, being among the heaviest buyers of Liberty Bonds among the foreign-speaking groups.[13] Since 1920 they have taken part in American civic life about as much as any well-organized immigrant group. The citizens' clubs occasionally participate in a body in large community political meetings. Ordinarily during an election campaign, however, they invite the American political leaders of all ranks, from the governor down to the ward boss, to speak to them, and at times there are so many speakers and political guests that they really could have a party caucus of their own. If such meetings are held in church buildings, as is often the case, the ladies of the congregation prepare a banquet for the occasion. Invariably there is some Ukrainian music which is followed by after-dinner speeches and political haranguing.

OFFICE-HOLDERS

In the years past the Ukrainian Americans have, for the most part, confined their political activity to the voting for others, but the sons of the immigrants, in ever increasing numbers, are seeking local and state offices. Thus far, three Ukrainian American lawyers have won seats in state legislatures: O. Malena in Pennsylvania in 1932, S. Jarema in New York in 1935, and John S. Gonas in Indiana in 1936. In Olyphant, Pennsylvania, a town of ten thousand people, nearly half of whom are Ukrainian, they succeeded in being elected to various city offices and even to the position of mayor, which George Chylak held from 1925 to 1930. On February 26, 1925, Governor Jackson of Indiana appointed Michael Havran as judge of the municipal court of East Chicago. He was later elected in his own name in November, 1925, for a four-year term, and then re-elected in November, 1929, for another term.[14] In 1935, in Arnold, Pennsylvania, two Ukrainians were on the school board, and several others held small local offices. In 1933 a Ukrainian also served on the school board in Wilton, North Dakota, and in the rural regions of that state scores of Ukrainians serve in like capacities. Aside from that, the past Ukrainian participation in American politics has been rather inconspicuous. They have not produced any political bosses.

Through the units of the American Legion and the Veterans of the World War thousands of Ukrainian Americans likewise come in contact with American organized life. Rev. Fr. Voloschuk of Johnston, Pennsylvania, held the state post of chaplain in the American Legion. In Philadelphia and New York they are organized into their own units. Also, there are several Ukrainian local labor unions that are affiliated with the American Federation of Labor, particularly in Pennsylvania and New York. Besides this group activity, hundreds of individuals belong to American organizations in several states.

CIVIC ACTIVITIES

The Ukrainian American public has reached the point where it is becoming more American numerically than Ukrainian. That means there is a larger number of those who were brought to America in their childhood or were born here than those who came as adult immigrants. Their most common participation in American community activities is on such occasions as Armistice Day, the Fourth of July, dedications and anniversaries commemorating some local or state historical event, and benefits for charity. At such times it is the church choirs and folk-dancing groups attired in their colorful native costumes that take part; in the case of a parade, the masses join also. Although the American public does not understand a word of Ukrainian, it likes Ukrainian folk songs and calls for more. On divers occasions both the general public and the music experts awarded Ukrainian singers with the highest honors possible, especially in Boston and Chicago. The Ukrainian groups have also served several times as entertainers for French, Lithuanian, and Norwegian Americans.[15] During the year beginning July 16, 1931, and ending July 20, 1932, eighteen stations in different cities broadcast one hundred and twenty-three Ukrainian programs, the most frequent being those of the Surma Book and Music Company of New York City.[16]

THE CHOIRS AND FOLK-DANCING GROUPS

There are several good Ukrainian mixed choirs, but not all are equally active. The most distinguished group during 1929–36 was the Ukrainian Orthodox Church Club of Boston, which was under the able leadership of Rev. Joseph Zelechevsky and in-

REV. JOSEPH ZELECHIVSKY AND HIS UKRAINIAN NATIONAL CHOIR
OF BOSTON, MASSACHUSETTS, 1935

cluded both a mixed choir and folk dancers. It participated in different American festivals along with other immigrant groups. Its first appearance, which was in connection with the celebration of the Tercentenary of Boston, was before an audience estimated at eighteen thousand. Following its initial appearance, the club received frequent requests for appearances in various activities in Boston. In 1930 this group won two first prizes in contests with other racial groups: one for embroidery in the international exhibit of handicraft and the other for the most beautiful costumes at the Boston Tercentenary Colonial Costume Ball. In 1932 the same group gave a concert at the estate of Mrs. C. Griggs Plant for the benefit of the Children's Sunlight Hospital. During the seven years of its existence the Ukrainian Orthodox Church Club of Boston gave twelve concerts and dancing performances before large American audiences, several concerts in American churches, and also broadcast over the Yankee Network of N.E. from WAAB, WNAC, and WBZ.[17]

In 1931 the mixed choir and Avramenko folk-dancing pupils of Elizabeth, New Jersey, participated in two contests with other nationalities and on both occasions were awarded the first place.[18] The mixed choir of the Ukrainian Presbyterian Church of Newark, New Jersey, under the direction of George Kirichenko, gained much popularity among the American people from the concerts it gave in various Protestant churches. In 1932 the Ukrainian amateur folk-dancing club of Milwaukee participated with the immigrant groups of other nationalities in a contest at the Wisconsin Theater, which was sponsored by the *Milwaukee Sentinel*. The Ukrainians won the contest. Out of the ten different Ukrainian churches in Pittsburgh, there always is an outstanding choir that takes part in community activities, either on the stage or over the radio. Also the choirs of the Ukrainian churches in Minneapolis, Detroit, and Cleveland have appeared before the American public in recent years, especially with native Christmas carols. For several years a choir of the Ukrainian Orthodox Church at Coatesville, Pennsylvania, likewise appeared before the American public in numerous concerts. As long as its director, Rev. Fr. Dmytryk, was in good health, the choir was the most noted among the Ukrainian choirs in the eastern part of that state. In 1931 it appeared in two charity programs, one at the United States Veterans' Hospital, the other at the benefit for the Coatesville fire department, the latter drawing close to seven thousand people.[19] The same year the choir of the Ukrainian Orthodox Church of Lyndora, Pennsylvania, presented a program for the benefit of the needy war veterans in Butler County.[20]

Many of the members of the choirs and choruses are also members of the Avramenko schools of folk dancing; invariably the choirs and dancing groups stage their performances to supplement each other. In 1931, when the popularity of the Ukrainian folk dancing in America seemed to be at its peak, the Cleveland group staged a huge dancing festival, some five hundred persons participating in the contest which was held in a large public hall. The performances so impressed the American school children who saw them that they began to imitate the dances of the Ukraine on the school playgrounds. When the teachers noticed this, they accommodated the youngsters in several instances by offering lessons in Ukrainian folk dancing in the gymnasium classes, Ukrainian instructors assisting.[21]

THE CHORUSES

In the cities of Scranton, Rochester, Chicago, and Cleveland large choruses have been organized, each one of which, at one time or another, has gained much local popularity among both Ukrainians and Americans. In 1931 the Scranton Ukrainian chorus, under the direction of Vladimir Levitzky, sang several times before large audiences in Central High School auditorium, and when it appeared on November 9, in a charity program to help the unemployed, it sang to a capacity audience and received much praise for its good work.[22] When Leo Sorochinsky directed the choruses of Rochester, Chicago, and lately Cleveland, his singers acquired a perfection that won them high honors in musical contests among some of the best choruses in the country. The Chicago Ukrainian chorus won great fame, when in 1930 and 1931, under the direction of Sorochinsky, it took first

UKRAINIAN CHORUS OF CHICAGO, WITH ITS DIRECTOR, MR. GEORGE BENETZKY, FIRST PRIZE WINNER IN CHICAGO TRIBUNE MUSIC CONTEST, 1935

place in the Chicago music festival. In 1932 it again won first place in the annual festival, this time with George Benetzky directing.[23] In 1933 it received second place, but in 1934 it once more took first place out of thirty choruses that participated. No other chorus that has taken part in the Chicago music festival has such a remarkable record for a similar time. This group also took part in frequent Ukrainian celebrations, in all-Slavic music contests, and appeared in concerts in the Civic Opera House and over the National Broadcasting System. It even gave concerts in some of the large cities of Missouri and Kansas. The following quotation of a music critic substantiates the fact that the Ukrainians of Chicago made a name for themselves in the music world: "Chicago's music is more than 50 per cent dependent upon the foreign-born element of its population. Among all the European-American groups at work here the Ukrainians, with their chorus, take a very high place."[24]

WORK OF ALEXANDER KOSHETZ

Alexander Koshetz, now of New York, was a great factor in popularizing Ukrainian music in several countries of the world. With his Ukrainian Chorus he traveled four years and gave concerts in the music centers of Europe as well as the large cities of that continent and America. His highly talented musicians had the highest degree of perfection and received much praise from music critics wherever they went.[25] At times they sang before forty thousand people, or even more, as was the case in Mexico City. They were professional singers whom the short-lived Ukrainian republic sent abroad. After the conquest of the Ukraine by the Bolsheviks, the chorus of that country fell apart likewise. Some of its former members are directing different choirs in Ukrainian American churches; others sing over the radio, among them the niece of Alexander Koshetz; still others joined several Russian singing groups and are advertised as "Russians."

In 1932, on the occasion of the Washington Bicentennial, Koshetz attempted to revive and reorganize his chorus but gathered a much smaller group, about thirty-five singers, with which he traveled in several states, giving concerts before a mixed Ukrainian and American public. Avramenko and his dancing school accompanied the chorus on its tour and appeared jointly

PROFESSOR ALEXANDER KOSHETZ

on the program. Koshetz and his chorus again received much praise from the music critics but met with financial deficits. Since then, as much as his health permitted, he has devoted his time to the composition of Ukrainian music and the arranging of some of it for English publication. By March, 1935, twenty

Ukrainian songs arranged by Koshetz had been published by Witmark Educational Publications in New York.[26] On the occasion of the 1935 convention of music teachers and critics of the North Central states, which was held in Indianapolis, Alexander Koshetz was invited to listen to the singing of Ukrainian songs as arranged by him in English. After hearing the singing directed by American leaders, he was given forty singers whom he trained himself and used to demonstrate how particular Ukrainian songs should sound in English.[27] In the spring of 1936 Koshetz directed the Ukrainian mixed choirs of the Metropolitan New York area in a first concert in Ukrainian church music. It was a success.

YOUNG COMPOSERS

Besides Koshetz, Roman Prydatkevich, a violinist and composer, traveled with his trio, giving concerts in Ukrainian music to college students. This "Ukrainian Trio," which consisted of Prydatkevich himself, Maria Hrehenetska, soprano, and Olga Tkachuk, pianist, invaded the campuses of the leading colleges and the State University of North Carolina in their tour of the southeastern states in 1930–31. The southerners gave the guests a cordial reception and were in turn well pleased with the programs.[28]

A third post-war immigrant-composer is Michael Hayvoronsky, who specializes in folk songs, particularly in military songs. A fourth Ukrainian American composer of importance is Paul Pecheniha-Uhlitzky, whose new compositions were played for an hour over the National Broadcasting System from New York, October 10, 1935.[29]

EFFORTS TO MAINTAIN UKRAINIAN OPERA

Following the World War so many professional musicians, former opera singers of the Ukraine, found themselves in exile that those of New York formed an organization in 1924 called "The Ukrainian Theater of New York," consisting of over thirty experienced singers. The organization, however, did not last long. In 1932 Dimitry Chutro organized a Ukrainian opera in Philadelphia, assembling the outstanding Ukrainian operatic talent in America and presenting the Ukrainian operas, "Zaporo-zhetz za Dunayem" ("The Cossack beyond the Danube") and Tchaikovsky's "Mazeppa." The organization had a successful 1932–33 season. The newspapers, both American and Ukrain-ian, made favorable comments in regard to the high quality of the operatic singing and "the dynamic folk dances" of Chutro's Ukrainian ballet.[30]

PARTICIPATION IN ART EXHIBITS

Besides their participation in divers social and musical activi-ties, the Ukrainians have been taking part in art exhibits in

PRIVATE COLLECTION OF UKRAINIAN FOLK ART OWNED
BY MR. JOSEPH KOCHAN, JOLIET, ILLINOIS

Boston, Stamford, New York, Jersey City, Newark (N.J.), Buf-falo, Cleveland, Chicago, St. Paul, Inglewood (Calif.), Houston (Tex.), Youngstown, and a few smaller towns. The art that they exhibit is not the work of professionally trained artists but the creation of the people as a whole. It consists of such crafts as textiles, decorated Easter eggs, woodcarving and staining, wood inlaid with other woods or with metal and beads, pottery, and leather-work. The most outstanding Ukrainian art exhibit ever displayed in America was that at the World's Fair in Chicago in 1933. Although there was a building that bore the name "Ukraine," it was the only building in the nationality group that was not financed by some government. The Ukrainian pavilion was built and the project financed by small voluntary contributions of Ukrainian Americans, the leadership resting in the Chicago group. The emigrants from the Ukraine living in Czecho-Slovakia, France, Canada, Brazil, and Argentina also helped the cause by sending articles for display.[31]

UKRAINIAN PAVILION AT THE WORLD'S FAIR IN CHICAGO

The Ukrainian pavilion was recognized by various art experts as one of the most unique structures at the Fair and in a class with the Japanese pavilion and the Temple of Jehol. The articles on display in the building consisted of the works of noted professional Ukrainian artists as well as folk handicraft. Alexander Archipenko, the great Ukrainian American sculptor, contributed the most to the success of the Ukrainian pavilion. His works occupied one room and were valued at twenty-five thousand dollars. Forty-eight individuals and societies sent articles for display, some of them being for sale, others not. The greatest demand was for the embroidered articles and the woodwork. Soon after this Ukrainian needle-work was exhibited, its effect became apparent, some style designers having adopted it in simplified form. For several seasons afterward, its influence was noticed in the clothes of young American women. Several American educators were interested in the books and especially in the maps also on display. The pavilion had a small stage and open-air theater in which Ukrainian music and folk dances were presented twice daily for several weeks. A restaurant in one section of the building served Ukrainian food.[32] During its existence the pavilion attracted at least a half-million people; no one kept a record for the entire time. The Sunday afternoon of

UKRAINIAN PAVILION AT CENTURY OF PROGRESS, CHICAGO, 1933

Ukrainian week the author counted ninety-four people entering the building in one minute (2:23 P.M.). The pavilion was not a financial success, but it accomplished its purpose: it presented to the wide world a sample of Ukrainian culture.

NOTES FOR CHAPTER IX

1. Parish libraries contained, on an average, about 300 volumes of novels, plays, poetry, history, and 2 or 3 newspapers.

2. These church schools do not possess the facilities of the public schools. They are held in the church halls with all the children (in most cases) congregating in one room and are taught by one person on the order of the American rural school. The training they offer in Ukrainian is very elementary. The parents even have to bear much pressure upon their children to make them attend (*Svoboda, June 9 and 11, 1932; Narodna Vola [Scranton], September 5, 1931).

3. Also most of the other books these people buy or read in American city libraries are imported.

4. The liturgical language of the Greek Catholic churches is the Old Slavonic, which the worshipers do not understand. The liturgy of many Ukrainian Orthodox churches is in native Ukrainian. All the churches, however, often supplement their services with religious songs in the vernacular. A few additional facts may be obtained from a pamphlet by Rev. Lev I. Sembratovich, Strangers within Our Gates (Detroit, 1936).

5. *Dnipro (Philadelphia), August 15, 1936.

6. According to the German critic F. M. Bodenstedt, "The Ukrainian language is the most melodious among all the Slavic tongues, having great musical properties" (Rev. Humphrey Kowalsky, Ukrainian Folk Songs [Boston, 1925], pp. 64–65).

7. Kowalsky's book (ibid.) contains a very extensive bibliography in several European languages on the Ukrainian folk songs.

8. Alexander Koshetz witnessed much of it on his last trip to Europe in 1932 and, upon his return to America, revealed the facts to the editors of the Ukrainian paper (*Svoboda, December 9, 1932).

9. On the 1932 United States Olympic team were the two Ukrainian Americans, Halaiko, a boxer, and Kojac, a great swimmer. The 1936 team had Peter Fick, likewise a swimmer.

10. Among the lecturers were several Detroit high-school teachers and one professor of the University of Michigan.

11. *Svoboda, October 2, 1935.

12. Michailo Pavlyk, "Ruthenians in America," *Tovarysh (Lwów), June 14, 1888, p. 38.

13. Literary Digest, LXIII (November 15, 1919), 40.

14. *Svoboda, November 17, 1932; letter from George Chylak to the author, August 26, 1936; letter from Michael Havran to the author, August 31, 1936.

15. *Svoboda, November 4, 1932.

16. The data on radio programs were compiled on the basis of the reports and announcements in the Ukrainian papers.

* The works indicated by asterisks are in Ukrainian.

17. Rev. Fr. Joseph Zelechivsky published a pamphlet in the spring of 1936 (no date of publication), which has a brief account of the social work of the Ukrainian Orthodox Holy Trinity Church, 136 Arlington Street, Boston.

18. *Svoboda*, June 17, 1931; *Elizabeth Journal*, June 18, 1931.

19. *Ukrainian Herald* (Carteret, N.J.), November 1931; *Coatesville Record*, October 2, 1931.

20. *Butler Eagle* (Butler, Pa.), December 12, 1931.

21. *Cleveland News*, June 9, 1931. The author is also indebted for the information to Rev. M. Zaparyniuk.

22. *Scranton Times*, November 10, 1931; *Scranton Republican*, November 10, 1931.

23. The Ukrainian Chorus of Chicago received considerable comment from the newspaper music critics: *Chicago Daily Tribune*, August 23, 1931; and May 9 and August 8, 1932; *Chicago Herald and Examiner*, May 9, 1932.

24. Eugene Stinson, *Chicago Daily News*, May 9, 1932.

25. Following the concert of the Ukrainian National Chorus at the Hippodrome, one music critic wrote: "The praise that preceded the chorus from all the musical centers of Europe seemed excessive until one heard it, until one saw Alexander Koshetz with his extraordinary living hands mold the sound as a sculptor molds the pliant clay. Here was that noblest and austerest and most stringently moral thing in the world—perfection."

26. A critical review of Koshetz' first few songs in English was written by Will Earhart, *Music Supervisor's Journal* (Pittsburgh), October, 1933.

27. S. Demydchuk, "Accomplishment of Professor Koshetz at a Music Conference," *Svoboda*, March 30, 1935.

28. *Durham Morning Herald*, July 2, 1931; *Daily Reflector* (Greenville, N.C.), July 3, 1931; *Svoboda*, November 17, 1931.

29. *Svoboda*, November 13, 1935.

30. Ukrainian papers: *America* (Philadelphia), May 24, 1932; *Svoboda*, November 22, 1932, and February 2, 1933. American papers: *New York Times*, February 5, 1933; *Evening News* (Buffalo), February 11, 1933.

31. A complete list of the artists and the articles they sent for exhibition in the Ukrainian pavilion appeared in the *Svoboda*, July 21, 1933.

32. V. Levitzky, "Ukrainian Participation in the Chicago Fair," *Almanac of the Ukrainian Workingmen's Association* (Scranton, Pa.), 1935, pp. 129–36.

CHAPTER X

CONCLUSION

ALTHOUGH many of the Ukrainian immigrants came to the United States with the intention of remaining here several years, earning a few hundred dollars, and returning to their native land, as the years elapsed only a small percentage found themselves back among their relatives in Europe as they had planned. In many cases, after they arrived there, they found no prospect of making a living and speedily endeavored to get back to America. Among those who did remain there permanently there has always been much discontent, for they often had to accept for the rest of their lives poorer living than they experienced during their stay on this side of the Atlantic.

It was really the World War that altered the plans of most of those who hoped to return to Europe. In the closing years of that struggle the Ukrainians had high hopes of seeing their country free from foreign despotic domination. They rejoiced as they read the proclamation of Wilson's Fourteen Points and the Declaration of Ukrainian Independence. But, as the world knows, the rising star of freedom did not rise very high for this nationality. Of all the peoples of Europe that were afflicted with the war, the Ukrainians have suffered the most. They were dealt with very unjustly by the nations for whom they fought as well as by their neighbors. Furthermore, they are the only large European nationality of over forty million people that does not possess independence. Thus by 1919 all hopes of returning to Europe permanently vanished from the minds of 98 per cent of the Ukrainian Americans. With their country partitioned by its four immediate neighbors, the foreign rulers of three of them each trying to outdo the others in oppressing the Ukrainian inhabitants, it is no wonder that those Ukrainians who found themselves in America concluded that they were better off in every way than their brethren in the native country and decided they were here for good. Of course, a great majority would have stayed here even had the Ukraine preserved its independence, just as have remained those other peoples living in America— Lithuanians, Esthonians, Latvians, Finns, and Czecho-Slovak- ians—whose countries won their independence as a result of the World War. Unaware of the fact, they were slowly taking root. America with its privileges and its freedom, they felt, was the best country for them.

Whether they are the best people for America, their past record and future actions will decide. Their social and economic im- provement, although a slow, hard climb, has been a steady one. In this, it must be admitted, they were handicapped. "Unlike the other nationalities who upon coming here found many of their countrymen occupying positions of power and influence, the Ukrainians had no one to extend to them a helping hand."[1] While they have much to learn from this country, they also have something to contribute. As has been pointed out before, they are hard-working, thrifty, and have no police record. Professor Andrew Mykytiak has characterized the Ukrainians as "senti- mental, contemplative, and restrained"[2] in their mental activity, while Allen H. Eaton came to the following conclusion after studying the social life among the recent immigrants:

In our search for immigrant gifts, sometimes the most interesting and color- ful are found among the late arrivals. To me, one of the most picturesque of our rather recent immigrant groups is from the Ukraine. Their entertainments are full of vivid action and beauty, and not the least charming thing about them is the way in which all the family take part, from the smallest children to the grandparents.[3]

Although not all of them are United States citizens yet, the percentage of noncitizens among them has been fast decreasing since 1920. They have about two hundred thousand American voters. A vast majority of them have lived in this country longer than in the land of their birth. Many own homes; they have like- wise helped to establish and maintain churches, lodges, benevo- lent associations, citizenship clubs, schools, and the press; their children and grandchildren were born here. They are all here to stay. The elders are trying to learn what they can about

Courtesy of Ukrainian National Association, publishers of "Jubilee Book"

UKRAINIAN DANCERS

America; simultaneously, many of them are anxious that their children learn about the best of Ukrainian culture in order that they may contribute something valuable to the great edifice—American civilization.

The Ukrainian Americans, as well as Americans of other non-English racial antecedents, have made certain contributions toward the development of this country, particularly along industrial lines. Those of the "old stock" can now be of assistance to them, if they will, in aiding them in the solution of their social problems. The immigrants themselves, as a rule, remain in the environment that they have created, but the second and third generations often face the necessity of social adjustment, as the institutions of their fathers do not always satisfy them. The Americans of the "old stock" can help by being more tolerant of their background, their non-Americanized surnames, and their slowly disappearing non-English institutions, and by extending a welcoming hand to those who wish to enter their social life. If both groups display the same spirit of co-operation and responsibility that characterized America during the World War and is still practiced in the field of amateur-sport competition, they will go a long way in creating, together, a better understanding, which will, in turn, result in a better Americanism.

The civic necessity of America was most aptly expressed in recent years by Calvin Coolidge when he said:

If we are to have that harmony and tranquillity, that union of spirit which is the foundation of real national genius and national progress, we must all realize that there are true Americans who did not happen to be born in our section of the country, who do not attend our place of religious worship, who are not of our racial stock, or who are not proficient in our language. If we are to create on this continent a free Republic and an enlightened civilization that will be capable of reflecting the true greatness and glory of mankind, it will be necessary to regard these differences as accidental and unessential. We shall have to look beyond the outward manifestations of race and creed. Divine Providence has not bestowed upon any race a monopoly of patriotism and character.[4]

NOTES FOR CHAPTER X

1. *Jubilee Book* (Jersey City, 1936), p. 493.
2. Trans. of Osyp Turiansky's *Lost Shadows* (New York, 1935), trans. n.
3. *Immigrant Gifts to American Life* (New York, 1932), p. 22.
4. From a speech, "Toleration and Liberalism," delivered before the American Legion Convention at Omaha, Nebraska, October 6, 1925. (*Foundation of the Republic, Speeches and Addresses* [New York and London, 1926], p. 299).

APPENDIX A*

DISTRIBUTION OF UKRAINIAN IMMIGRANTS IN THE UNITED STATES
AT THE TIME OF THEIR ARRIVAL

(The following states were their destination)

Year	Ala.	Alaska	Ariz.	Ark.	Calif.	Colo.	Conn.	Del.
1899	.....	.....	.....	3	.....	4	70	.....
1900	.....	.....	.....	.....	19	25	111	3
1901	3	.....	.....	.....	1	.....	132	8
1902	2	.....	.....	.....	.....	5	195	8
1903	1	.....	.....	5	.....	3	213	12
1904	6	.....	.....	4	10	6	255	25
1905	.....	.....	.....	.....	2	3	362	21
1906	.....	.....	.....	.....	21	1	426	68
1907	1	1	.....	.....	45	17	765	110
1908	2	.....	.....	.....	3	44	218	48
1909	1	.....	2	.....	9	5	433	68
1910	9	2	.....	.....	3	5	824	143
1911	1	1	.....	.....	11	24	465	56
1912	.....	.....	.....	.....	13	6	741	74
1913	1	.....	2	.....	10	5	988	212
1914	1	4	4	.....	15	9	1,079	139
1915	.....	16	.....	.....	4	1	67	5
1916	.....	.....	.....	.....	3	3	15	.....
1917	.....	.....	.....	.....	37	.....	14	.....
1918	.....	.....	.....	.....	1	.....	.....	.....
1919	1	.....	.....	.....	.....	.....	1	.....
1920	.....	.....	.....	.....	2	.....	2	.....
1921–30	2	2	1	.....	191	7	121	9
Total by states	31	26	9	12	400	173	7,498	1,009

* Statistical data taken from the annual reports of the commissioner of immigration, 1899–1930. They represent the destination as given by the immigrants at the ports of entry. Owing to the fact that many Ukrainian immigrants were registered Russians and Austrians, the foregoing may not be considered complete.

Year	D.C.	Fla.	Ga.	Hawaii	Idaho	Ill.	Ind.	Indian Terr.
1899						13	1	
1900	2					66	5	
1901						146	3	1
1902						111	9	
1903	2					193	25	6
1904	1				1	199	9	4
1905	1					230	22	8
1906						407	28	5
1907		3			2	601	39	40
1908					2	374	26	6
1909						525	46	
1910	1					922	85	
1911					5	647	71	
1912	1	2			4	823	96	
1913	7	4			3	1,275	185	
1914	2	1			6	1,871	219	
1915					2	104	14	
1916	1	1			3	44	1	
1917		2			4	69	6	
1918	1					2		
1919								
1920						6		
1921–30	2	46	2	1	5	1,457	83	
Total by states	21	59	2	1	36	10,085	973	70

Year	Iowa	Kan.	Ky.	La.	Me.	Md.	Mass.	Mich.	Minn.
1899				4			31	4	3
1900		31				11	125	22	10
1901	1	2				12	230	25	14
1902					4	18	176	16	17
1903	1			2		37	220	36	21
1904	3	6		1	1	56	156	40	20
1905	3	5	3		5	79	232	51	41
1906	6	4	1			104	353	53	55
1907	1	7		22	9	263	564	164	117
1908	7	38		51	9	58	342	101	127
1909	8	5		4	15	49	516	137	181
1910	7	6	1	3	21	60	660	208	177
1911	10	17		1	7	76	552	206	136
1912	20	37		1	12	59	627	298	173
1913	15	28	1	1	22	73	965	729	308
1914	20	30	3		48	178	1,336	1,009	584
1915		1	1		5	6	135	470	137
1916	5				4	1	47	297	238
1917	1	1			1	1	4	234	154
1918				1				10	8
1919						2		15	5
1920							6	36	15
1921–30	7	1		7	5	20	110	1,487	755
Total by states	115	219	10	99	168	1,163	7,357	5,648	3,296

Year	Miss.	Mo.	Mont.	Neb.	Nev.	N.H.	N.J.	N.M.
1899		9	1			2	257	
1900	1	14				10	359	
1901		30		4		22	621	
1902	1	39	7	1		10	746	
1903		44	1	3		22	874	
1904		43		1		24	1,094	
1905	2	101				23	1,666	1
1906	1	131	2	1		44	1,692	
1907	4	267	11	1		81	2,714	
1908		120	1	3		40	1,182	
1909		131	7	11		66	2,136	
1910		207	33	12		88	3,274	
1911	1	149	52	11		51	2,247	
1912		195	82	16		96	2,889	
1913	3	227	52	13		159	3,327	1
1914		367	27	22		243	4,046	2
1915	1	29	22			11	267	
1916		1	30	4		3		
1917		5	14	1		2	11	
1918		1	3					
1919		3	2			1	7	
1920		1	2				9	
1921–30	1	73	52	6	1	8	422	
Total by states	15	2,187	400	108	1	1,006	29,830	4

Year	N.Y.	N.C.	N.D.	Ohio	Okla.	Ore.	Pa.	P.I.
1899	339		5	27			608	
1900	560		22	54		1	1,332	
1901	967		15	132			2,854	
1902	1,594		21	328			4,133	
1903	1,854		1	391			5,675	
1904	1,653		48	405			5,336	
1905	2,275	1	19	522			8,510	
1906	3,626		61	552		5	8,243	
1907	5,090		78	671		4	11,779	
1908	3,318	1	119	396	4	3	5,229	
1909	4,085		96	435	4	7	6,364	
1910	5,946		100	1,071	7	18	13,386	
1911	4,991		66	564	8	4	6,902	
1912	5,982		308	848	7	41	7,909	
1913	7,642	2	79	1,467	22	5	12,007	
1914	9,961		107	1,526	10	11	12,937	2
1915	578		61	73	3	3	784	
1916	227		148	61		16	81	
1917	194		128	214		6	54	
1918	8		3			2	1	
1919	36		1	7		5	10	
1920	105		4	6		4	42	
1921–30	1,183	3	89	409	13	61	1,192	
Total by states	62,214	7	1,579	10,169	78	196	114,179	2

Year	R.I.	S.C.	S.D.	Tenn.	Tex.	Utah	Vt.	Va.
1899	4						1	2
1900	9				4		6	
1901	15				12		8	10
1902	15				1		23	14
1903	41				10	1	51	8
1904	50				16		44	2
1905	63		2		25		65	17
1906	84		2		124		51	6
1907	193	3	1		166		43	13
1908	143		11		136		22	3
1909	171	2	16		42		64	9
1910	187		2		53	1	63	10
1911	108		5	1	70		26	11
1912	247			1	38	1	46	15
1913	337		1	3	51		33	22
1914	329	7	1	2	63	1	42	25
1915	18				8		7	8
1916			1					3
1917			1	16	1			1
1918								
1919			1					4
1920	2							5
1921–30	25		3	1	3	2	4	24
Total by states	2,041	12	47	24	823	6	599	210

Year	Wash.	W.Va.	Wis.	Wyo.	Total
1899		6	6		1,400
1900	18	9	3		2,832
1901	1	13	6		5,288
1902	3	28	5	3	7,533
1903		71	18	1	9,843
1904	8	42	17	6	9,592
1905	6	75	29	3	14,473
1906	4	74	20	2	16,257
1907	53	114	20	4	24,081
1908	42	75	57		12,361
1909	39	84	34	1	15,808
1910	25	166	115	6	27,907
1911	39	98	31	3	17,724
1912	14	187	56		21,965
1913	12	201	83	2	30,588
1914	60	252	121	5	36,527
1915	49	19	24		2,933
1916	60	4	9		1,365
1917	22		13		1,211
1918	4		4		49
1919	2				103
1920	8		2		258
1921–30	104	69	122	8	8,213
Total by states	573	1,587	795	44	268,311
1931–36					587
Grand total					268,898

APPENDIX B

California:
  Los Angeles
  San Francisco

Colorado:
  Denver
  Pueblo
  Ramah

District of Columbia:
  Washington

Connecticut:
  Ansonia
  Bethel
  Bridgeport
  Bristol
  Chesterfield
  Colchester
  Coscob
  Danbury
  Derby
  Fairfield
  Forestville
  Glastonbury
  Glenville
  Hartford
  Meriden
  New Britain
  New Haven
  Norwich
  North Miamus
  Orange
  Oxford
  Seymour
  Southport
  Stafford
  Stamford

  Stratford
  Terryville
  Thomaston
  Wallingford
  Willimantic

Delaware:
  Wilmington

Illinois:
  Benton
  Calumet City
  Chicago
  Christopher
  Cicero
  East St. Louis
  Elmwood Park
  Harvey
  Joliet
  Madison
  Melrose Park
  Mount Olive
  Peoria
  Phoenix
  West Hammond
  Witt
  Zeigler

Indiana:
  East Chicago
  Gary
  Hammond
  South Bend
  Whiting

Iowa:
  Lovilia
  Oelwein
  Sioux City

154

APPENDIX B—*Continued*

Kansas:
Kansas City

Louisiana:
New Orleans

Maryland:
Baltimore
Chesapeake City
Curtis Bay
Locust Point

Massachusetts:
Amherst
Attleboro
Boston
Cambridge
Chicopee Falls
Fall River
Farmers
Gardner
Holyoke
Lawrence
Ludlow
Matapan
Medford
New Bedford
Pittsfield
Salem
Shelburne
South Deerfield
Taunton

Michigan:
Bay City
Dearborn
Detroit
Flint
Fosters
Fruitport
Grand Rapids
Hamtramck
Ironwood
Lansing
Muskegon

Muskegon Heights
Pinconning
Saginaw
Saline

Minnesota:
Barnum
Chisholm
Duluth
Hibbing
Minneapolis
Osseo
Royalton
St. Paul

Missouri:
Desloge
St. Francis
St. Joseph
St. Louis

Montana:
Anaconda
Butte
Giltedge
Great Meadows
Larslan
Miles City
Sand Creek
Scobey
Stockett

New Hampshire:
Hinsdale
Manchester

New Jersey:
Bayonne
Blairstown
Bound Brook
Bridgeton
Camden
Carlstad
Carteret
Clifton
Dunellen

APPENDIX B—*Continued*

New Jersey—Continued:

East Orange
Elizabeth
Fords
Garfield
Great Meadows
Harrison
Irvington
Iselin
Jersey City
Johnsonburg
Lincoln
Linden
Little Falls
Lodi
Manville
Maplewood
Millville
Newark
New Brunswick
Newton
New Market
Nova Ukraina
Oxford Furnace
Paterson
Passaic
Paulsboro
Perth Amboy
Phillipsburg
Plainfield
Plainsboro
Rahway
Raritan
Rockaway
Roebling
Roselle
Rutherford
Scotch Plains
South Plainfield
Trenton
Union
Wallington

Whippany
Williamstown
Woodbine

New York:

Amsterdam
Astoria, L.I.
Auburn
Babylon
Bath
Binghamton
Broadalbin
Brooklyn
Buffalo
Churchville
Cohoes
Corning
Durhamville
East Hempstead
Elmira
Elmira Heights
Elmont
Endicott
Fulton
Far Rockaway, L.I.
Galway
Glenfield
Granville
Hastings-on-Hudson
Hempstead
Herkimer
Hicksville
Hornell
Hudson
Irondequoit
Jamaica, L.I.
Johnson City
Lackawanna
Lancaster
Lee Center
Little Falls
Long Island City
Manchester

APPENDIX B—*Continued*

Mattituck
New York
Niagara Falls
Olean
Ozon Park, L.I.
Peekskill
Port Jervis
Prattsburg
Reine
Richmond Hill
Riverhead, L.I.
Rochester
Rome
Roslyn, L.I.
Saint Johnsville
Spring Valley
Stapleton
Syracuse
Troy
Utica
Watervliet
Westbury, L.I.
Westchester
Whiteston, L.I.
Woodhaven
Yonkers

North Dakota:
Backoo
Belfield
Benedict
Butte
Caledonia
Casselton
Douglas
Fayette
Fredonia
Fried
Fryburg
Gorham
Grassy Butte
Kief
Killdeer

Kongsberg
Makoti
Mary
Max
Minot
New Hradec
Oakdale
Pembina
Raleigh
Ruso
Ryder
Snow
Ukraina
Williston
Wilton

Ohio:
Akron
Ashtabula
Barberton
Barton
Belle Valley
Blaine
Byesville
Campbell
Canton
Cleveland
East Youngstown
Empire
Fairport Harbor
Girard
Kipling
Lakewood
Lorain
Marblehead
Masury
Mingo
Newton Falls
Niles
Pleasant City
Rossford
Struthers
Toledo

APPENDIX B—*Continued*

Ohio—Continued:
Toronto
Warren
Yorkville
Youngstown
Zanesville

Oklahoma:
Harrah
Hartshorne
Henryetta
Jones
Prague

Oregon:
Eugene
Portland

Pennsylvania:
Albion
Alden Station
Aliquippa
Allentown
Allison
Altoona
Ambridge
Amerald
Arcadia
Ardmore
Arnold
Ashley
Atlas
Avella
Avoca
Baggaley
Barnsboro
Bath
Beaver
Beaverdale
Beaver Meadows
Bellefonte
Bentleyville
Berwick
Bethlehem
Bitumen

Black Lick
Brackenridge
Braddock
Bradenville
Bradford
Breslau
Bridgeport
Bristol
Brockton
Brownsville
Burgettstown
Butler
California
Canonsburg
Carbondale
Carnegie
Central City
Centralia
Charleroi
Chester
Clairton
Clarence
Clifton Heights
Clymer
Coaldale
Coalrun
Coatesville
Colver
Conemaugh
Cuddy
Culpmont
Delano
Derry
Dickson
Dixonville
Donora
Doylestown
Dunlo
Dunmore
Duquesne
Duryea
East Pittsburgh

APPENDIX B—*Continued*

Easton
Eckley
Edwardsville
Egypt
Emerald
Erie
Etna
Evansville
Everson
Export
Farrell
Forbes Road
Ford City
Frackville
Frankford
Freeland
Glassport
Glen Lyon
Glenwood
Grassmere
Hannastown
Hanover
Hawk Run
Hazelton
Hermenie
Homer City
Homestead
Hostetter
Houtzdale
Iselin
Jeanette
Jenners
Jerome
Jessup
Johnstown
Keiser
Kimberton
Kingston
Koppel
Kumbola
Lansford
Latrobe

Leechburg
Leetsdale
Leisenring
Lilly
Linfield
Llewelyn
Lopez
Ludlow
Lundys Lane
Lyndora
McAdoo
McKeesport
McKees Rocks
Magaley
Mahanoy City
Mahanoy Plane
Maizeville
Maltby
Manifold
Manayoung
Mar Lin
Mayfield
Middleport
Middletown
Millville
Minersville
Monessen
Monongahela
Mont Claire
Moscow
Mount Carmel
Mount Union
Nanticoke
Nanty Glo
Nesquehoning
New Alexandria
New Castle
New Kensington
New Salem
Newville
Nicetown
Northampton

APPENDIX B—*Continued*

Pennsylvania—Continued:

Northumberland
Norwich
Oakland
Oil City
Old Forge
Olyphant
Ormrod
Palmerton
Parkford
Parnassus
Parsons
Patton
Perryopolis
Philadelphia
Phoenixville
Pittsburgh
Pittston
Plains
Plainsboro
Plymouth
Portage
Portvue
Pottstown
Punxsutawney
Quakertown
Ramey
Rankin
Reading
Revloc
Rhone
Roscoe
Russellton
Sagamore
St. Clair
Sayre
Scranton
Scott
Scottdale
Sewickley
Shamokin

Sharon
Sheffield
Shenandoah
Sheppton
Simpson
Skippack
Slickville
Smith Mill
Smoke Run
South Fork
Southwest
Spangler
Swayersville
Sykesville
Taylor
Thompson
Titusville
Tower City
Trascow
Trauger
Uniontown
Vandergrift
Van Voorhis
Verona
Vintondale
Wall
Washington
Waterman
Webster
West Eaton
West Newton
West Park
West Terentum
Wilkes-Barre
Williamstown
Wilmerding
Wilpen
Windber
Woodland
Yatesboro
Yukon

APPENDIX B—*Continued*

Rhode Island:
  Central Falls
  Crompton
  Manville
  Newport
  Pawtucket
  Providence
  West Warwick
  Woonsocket

Texas:
  Bremond
  Dundee
  Fort Worth
  Houston
  Marlin
  New Waverly
  Schulenburg

Washington:
  Tacoma
  Seattle

West Virginia:
  Algona
  Beech Bottom
  Benwood
  Clarksburg
  Elmhurst
  Factoryville
  Glen Dale
  McKeeferry
  Morgantown
  Sabraton
  Scarbo
  Tams
  Thomas
  Weirton
  Wheeling
  Windsor Heights

Wisconsin:
  Clayton
  Cornucopia
  Huron
  Kenosha
  Lublin
  Milwaukee
  Racine
  Superior
  Suring
  Thorp
  West Allis

Wyoming:
  Frontier
  Rock Spring
  Sublet

APPENDIX C

DISTRIBUTION OF UKRAINIAN AMERICANS IN THE UNITED STATES

Goode's Series of Base Maps (The University of Chicago Press, 1937)

BIBLIOGRAPHY

OFFICIAL DOCUMENTS

Abstract of the Fourteenth Census of the United States, 1920, Vol. XII.

Annual Reports of the Commissioner General of Immigration (1899–1930).

"Dictionary of Races or Peoples," *Senate Documents* (61st Cong., 3d sess.), Vol. IX. Washington, 1911.

"Distribution of Immigrants," *ibid.,* Vols. IX, XX, and LXIX.

"Emigration Conditions in Europe," *ibid.,* Vol. XII.

"Immigration Commission Abstract Reports," *ibid.,* Vols. VII and VIII. Washington, 1910–11.

"Immigration and Crime," *ibid.,* Vol. XVIII.

"Immigrants in Industries," *ibid.,* Vols. LXVIII, LXXI, LXXII, and LXXVIII.

"Immigrants in Manufacturing and Mining," *ibid.,* Vols. VII and LXXXII.

"Iron and Steel Manufacturing," *ibid.* (61st Cong., 2d sess.), Vols. LXX–LXXI. Washington, 1909–10.

ALMANACS, LETTERS, MANUSCRIPTS, AND MEMOIRS

*Almanac of Orphan's Home. Philadelphia, 1932–36.

*Almanac of the Providence Association. Philadelphia, 1912–33.

*Almanac of the Sojedinenija Ruthenian Greek Catholic Association. Homestead (Pa.), 1896–1934.

*Almanac of the Ukrainian National Aid Association. Pittsburgh, 1912–32.

*Almanac of the Ukrainian National Association. Jersey City, 1899–1933.

*Almanac of the Ukrainian Women's League of New York. New York, 1921–31.

*Almanac of the Ukrainian Workingmen's Association. Scranton, 1914–37 (esp. 1935–37).

BYCHINSKY, ANNA. "The Way of Ruth" (a story; MS). Ann Arbor.

*Collection of Letters in the possession of the author.

KUSIW, REV. BASIL. "Report of the Ukrainian Evangelical Church at the Prague Conference, September 25, 1936"(MS).

*Memoirs of Honcharenko. Kolomea, 1894.

*"Memoirs of the Rev. Alex Prystay" (MS). New Haven.

MONSTEIN, BARON DE, *Memoirs of Russia.* London, 1770.

REVYUK, EMIL. *Polish Atrocities in Ukraine.* New York, 1931.

Statutes and by-laws of the Ukrainian mutual aid associations (names and locations given above).

*Statutes of the Ukrainian Women's League of America. Jersey City, 1932.

VOLANSKY, REV. JOHN. "Memoirs of Olden Years," **Svoboda* (Jersey City), September 5, 1912.

* The works indicated by an asterisk are in Ukrainian.

163

SECONDARY WORKS

ABBOTT, EDITH. *Immigration: Select Documents and Case Records.* Chicago: University of Chicago Press, 1924.

ABBOTT, GRACE. *The Immigrant and the Community.* New York: Century Co., 1917.

*ANDRUCHOVICH, REV. CONSTANTINE. *Z zhitia Rusiniv v Americi.* ("From the Life of Ukrainians in America"). Kolomea, 1904.

*ARKAS, M. *History of Ukraine.* 3d ed. Leipzig, n.d.

BALCH, EMILY GREEN. *Our Slavic Fellow Citizens.* New York: Charities Publication Committee, 1910.

*BATCHINSKY, JULIAN. *Ukrainian Immigration in the United States of America.* Lwów: Julian Batchinsky & Ol. Harasevich, 1914.

Beauplan's Description of the Ukraine, I, 571–610.

BROWN, LAWRENCE GUY. *Immigration.* New York: Longmans, Green & Co., 1933.

BUTLER, RALPH. *The New Eastern Europe.* London: Longmans, Green & Co., 1919.

Churchill's Voyages: A Collection of Voyages and Travels of J. Churchill in Four Volumes. London, 1704.

CLARK, EDWARD DANIEL. *Travels in Various Countries of Europe, Asia and Africa,* Vol. I. 2d ed. London: T. Cadell & W. Davies, 1811.

COMMONS, JOHN R. *Races and Immigrants in America.* New York: Century Co., 1907.

CRESSON, WILLIAM P. *The Cossacks.* New York: Brentanos, 1919.

DAVIS, JEROME. *The Russian Immigrant.* New York: Macmillan Co., 1922.

———. *The Russians and Ruthenians in America.* New York: Doran, 1922.

DAVIS, PHILIP. *Immigration and Americanization.* Boston: Ginn & Co., 1920.

EATON, ALLEN H. *Immigrant Gifts to America.* New York: Russell Sage Foundation, 1932.

EVERSLEY, LORD, GEORGE. *The Turkish Empire from 1288 to 1914.* London: T. Fisher Unwin Ltd., 1924.

FAIRCHILD, HENRY P. *Immigrant Background.* New York: John Wilby & Sons, Inc., 1927.

FISHER, HAROLD H. *America and the New Poland.* New York: Macmillan Co., 1928.

GAMBAL, MARIE S. *The Story of Ukraine.* Scranton: Ukrainian Working Men's Association (n.d.).

GIBBONS, HERBERT ADAMS. *Europe since 1918.* New York: Century Co., 1926.

GROSS, HOWARD B. *Aliens or Immigrants.* Cincinnati: Jennings & Graham, 1906.

GUTHRIE, WILLIAM. *A New Geographical, Historical and Commercial Grammar: and Present State of the Several Kingdoms of the World.* London: J. Knox, 1770.

HALICH, WASYL. *Economic Aspects of Ukrainian Activities in the United States.* ("University of Iowa Studies," Abstracts in History, Vol. X, No. 3.) Iowa City, 1934.

HALL, PRESCOTT F. *Immigration.* New York: Henry Holt & Co., 1906.

*HNATIUK, VOLODIMIR. *The Baron's Son.* Kiev: Vernihora Co., 1917.

*HRUSHEVSKY, MICHAILO. *History of Ukraine.* Canadian ed. Winnipeg: Ukrainian Book Store, 1918.

————. *History of Ukraine,* Vol. VIII, Part III. Kiev and Lwów, 1905–22.

JENKS, J. W., and LAUCK, W. J. *The Immigration Problem.* New York: Funk & Wagnalls Co., 1913.

JONQUIERE, DE A. LA. *Histoire de l'Empire Ottoman.* Paris: Librairie Hachett et cie, 1914.

Jubilee Almanac of Ukrainian Greek Catholic Church. Philadelphia, 1934.

Jubilee Book. Jersey City: Ukrainian National Association, 1936.

*KIRILENKO, OREST. *Ukrainians in America.* Vienna: Sojuz Vizvolenia Ukrainy, 1916.

KIRK CONNELL, WATSON. *The European Heritage.* London and Toronto: J. M. Dent & Sons, 1930.

*KOROLENKO, VOLODIMIR. *Without a Language.* ("World Library.") Lwów, 1918.

*KOROLIV, VASILE. *Ukrainians in the United States.* Kiev, 1909.

KOWALSKY, HUMPHREY, *Ukrainian Folk Songs.* Boston: Stratford Co., 1925.

LORD, ROBERT H. *The Second Partition of Poland.* Cambridge: Harvard University Press, 1915.

MACAULEY, JAMES. *The Natural Statistical and Civil History of the State of New York.* Vol. II. Albany, 1829.

McCLURE, ARCHIBALD. *Leadership of the New America.* New York: George H. Doran Co., 1916.

MIRSKY, DIMITRY S. *Russia: A Social History.* London: Cresset Press, 1931.

ORTH, SAMUEL P. *Our Foreigners.* New Haven: Yale University Press, 1920.

*PRYSTAY, REV. ALEX. *From Truskavtzia to the World of Skyscrapers* (Memoirs), Vols. I, II, and III. Lwów and New York: By the author, 1933–37. (The first three volumes only were published, the others are in press.)

ROBERTS, PETER. *The New Immigrants.* New York: Macmillan Co., 1912.

————. *Immigrant Races in North America.* New York: Y.M.C.A. Press, 1910.

RUDNITZKY, STEPHAN. *Pochatkova Geografia.* Kiev: Vernihora Co., 1919.

————. *Ukraine: The Land and Its People.* New York, 1918.

————. *The Ukraine and Ukrainians.* Jersey City: Ukrainian National Council, 1915.

*SHELUKHIN, SERHEY. *Ukraina.* Praha, 1936.

*SICHINSKY, VOLODIMIR. *Ukrainian Wooden Architecture and Carvings.* Scranton, 1937.

STEINER, EDWARD A. *The Immigrant Tide: Its Ebb and Flow.* Revell, 1909.

STEPHENSON, GEORGE M. *A History of the American Immigration.* Boston: Ginn & Co., 1926.

STRONBERG, ANDREW A. *A History of Sveden.* New York: Macmillan Co., 1931.

TILTMAN, H. HESSEL. *Peasant Europe.* London: Jarrolds, Publishers, 1934.

TOOK (F.R.S.), WILLIAM. *View of the Russian Empire during the Reign of Catharine the Second.* 3 vols. London, 1800.

VERNARDSKY, G. *History of Russia.* New Haven: Yale University Press, 1929.

†VILCHUR, MARK. *Russians in America.* New York: First Russian Publishing Co., 1918.

WARNE, FRANK JULIAN. *The Slav Invasion and the Mine Workers.* Philadelphia and London: J. B. Lippincott, 1904.

WINTER, NEVIN O. *New Poland.* Boston: Page & Co., 1923.

———. *The Russian Empire of Today and Yesterday.* Boston: Page & Co., 1913.

*WOZNIAK, M. *The Statehood of Ukraine.* Vienna, 1918.

*YASINCHUK, LEV. *Za Oceanon* ("Beyond the Ocean"). Lwów: Ridna Shkola, 1930.

———. *Dla Ridnoho Krayon* ("For the Native Land"). Lwów: By the Author, 1933.

YOUNG, CHARLES H. *The Ukrainian Canadians.* Toronto: Thomas Nelson & Sons Limited, 1931.

PERIODICALS AND PAMPHLETS

ADAMIC, LOUIS. "Thirty Million New Americans," *Harper's Monthly Magazine,* November, 1934, pp. 684–94.

Album of Twenty-fifth Anniversary of Ukrainian Catholic Church of St. Nicholas. Watervliet, N.Y., 1932.

ARDAN, IVAN. "The Ruthenians in America," *Charities,* XIII (1904–5), 246–52.

BALCH, EMILY GREEN. "Slav Emigration and Its Sources," *Charities and Commons,* XVI (1906), 71–78, 171–83.

"Birth of the Ukrainian Republic," *Literary Digest,* LVI (February 23, 1918), 7–8.

BOSTON PUBLIC LIBRARY. Free Lectures and Concerts, 1931–32.

*BOYKA, S. "Ukrainian Churches in America." *Almanac Krinitzia,* Lwów, 1937, pp. 96–98.

BUCHAK, REV. LEO. "The New Protestant Movement," *Presbyterian,* June 18, 1931, pp. 11, 26–27.

CEGLINSKY, NICHOLAS. "How the Ukrainians Came," *The Interpreter* (published by the Foreign Language Information Service), January, 1924.

———. "Ukrainians in America," *ibid.,* December, 1924.

*CHYZ, Y. "Ukrainian Emigrants in Hawaii," *Almanac* (1936) *of the Ukrainian Workingmen's Association,* Scranton, 1935.

———. "Information about the Ukrainians in America before the Civil War," *Almanac* (1937) *of the Ukrainian Workingmen's Association,* Scranton, 1936, pp. 101–11.

† This work is in Russian.

COMMONS, J. R. "Slavs in Bituminous Mines of Illinois," *Charities and Commons*, XIII (December 3, 1904) 227–29.

———. "Wage Earners of Pittsburgh," *ibid.*, XXI (March 6, 1909), 1051–64.

DANYS, TEKLA. "Ukrainian Christmas," *San Francisco Teachers Bulletin*, December, 1934.

DAVIE, MENIE MURIER. "In Ruthenia," *Living Age*. CLXXXVII (November, 1890), 364–71.

DWULIT, REV. THEODOR. *Ukrainian Semi-annual*. South Deerfield, Mass., 1927. (This pamphlet contains some historical accounts but is very inaccurate.)

GIBBONS, HERBERT ADAMS. "The Ukraine and the Balance of Power," *Century Magazine*, July, 1921, pp. 463–71.

HALICH, WASYL. "Ukrainian Farmers in the United States," *Agricultural History*, January, 1936, pp. 25–39.

———. "Ukrainians in Western Pennsylvania," *Western Pennsylvania Historical Magazine*, June, 1935, pp. 139–46.

*HALKO, MICHAEL. "Spohadi Emigranta" ("Memoirs of the Emigrant"), *Almanac of the Ukrainian Workingmen's Association*, Scranton, 1935, pp. 63–69.

KOROSTOVETZ, VOLODIMIR. "The Ukrainian Problem," *Contemporary Review*, CXLI (June, 1932), 733–39.

LAUCK, W. J. "The Bituminous Coal Miner and Coke Worker in Western Pennsylvania," *Survey*, XXVI (April 1, 1911), 34–55.

LEES, GEORGE F. "The Literature of Ukrainia," *Living Age*, CCXCVIII, 752–55.

*LEVITZKY, V. "Ukrainian Participation in the Chicago Fair," *Almanac of the Ukrainian Workingmen's Association*, Scranton, 1935, pp. 129–36.

LLOYD, J. A. T. "Teuton versus Slav," *Fortnightly Review*, CV (May, 1916), 883–93.

McLAUGHLIN, ALLAN. "The Slavic Immigrant," *Popular Science Monthly*, LXIII (May, 1903), 25–32.

*MAKOVAY, OSSYP. "Dollari" ("Dollars"), *Almanac of Orphans' Home*, Philadelphia, 1936, pp. 112–25.

†MATROSOV, E. N. "Za Oceanska Rus" (Transoceanic Ruthenia"), *Istoricheskey Viestnik* ("Historical Herald"), St. Petersburg, 1897, Vol. LXXVIII.

"The New Republic of Rusinia, Mostly Made in America," *Literary Digest*, LXIX (June 25, 1921), 41–43.

*PAWLYK, MICHAILO, "Ukrainians in America," *Tovarysh*, Lwów, June 14, 1888, pp. 35–49.

*PETROVSKY, MICHAEL. "Po Amerikansky" (In American Way), *Ukrainian Bazaar* (Toronto, Can.), Vol. I, February and March, 1934.

REVYUK, EMIL. *Trade with the Ukraine*. Washington: Friends of Ukraine, 1920.

———. *Ukraine and Ukrainians*. Washington: Friends of Ukraine, 1920.

ROSS, EDWARD, A. "The Slavs in America," *Century*, LXXXVIII (August, 1914), 590–98.

"Rusinia," *Literary Digest*, LXIV (February 7, 1920), 42, 106–7.

SANDS, BEDWIN. "The Ukrainians and the War," *Contemporary Review*, CIX, 396–97.

SEMBRATOVICH, REV. LEO. *Strangers within Our Gates*. Detroit, 1936.

*SHELUKHIN, SERHEY. *The Name Ukraine*. Vienna: Franco Son & Co., 1921.

SHRIVER, WILLIAM P. *Immigrant Forces*. New York: Missionary Education Movement of the United States and Canada, 1913.

*SIMENOVICH, VLADIMIR. "Ukrainian Immigration in the United States," *Ukrainia*, Chicago, March 13, 1931.

"Songs of the Ukraine," *American Eclestic*, I (March, 1841), 332–51.

*"Souvenir of Twenty-fifth Anniversary of the Ukrainian Catholic Church of SS. Peter and Paul," Ambridge, Pa., and "Silver Jubilee of Ordination to Priesthood of Rev. Fr. Nicholas Kopachuk," Ambridge, n.d.

Tenth Anniversary of the Rev. Michael Guransky's Pastorate of St. Cyril Methodius Ukrainian Church. Olyphant, October 28, 1930.

"Those Who Enter without Knocking," *The Interpreter*, V (November, 1926), 3–7.

TICHENOR, GEORGE. "Ukrainia on the Bowery," *Theatre Arts Monthly*, XV, 515–25.

"Ukrainian and Bohemian Needle Work," *Ladies Home Journal*, XXXVIII (November, 1921), 32.

The Ukrainian Herald, passim. Carteret, N.J., 1933–34. (This publication is partly in Ukrainian, partly in English.)

Ukrainian Orthodox Church of America. New York: By the Consistory, 1931.

The Ukrainian Review, Vols. I–III. New York, 1931.

"Ukrainians in America," *Literary Digest*, LXIII (November 15, 1919), 40.

WINTER, NEVIN O. "The Ukraine, Past and Present," *National Geographic Magazine*, XXXVIII (August, 1918), 114–28.

Zinochy Svit (Pittsburgh), 1933.

NEWSPAPERS

‡*America*, Philadelphia, 1912–34.

Boston Evening Transcript, July, 1930.

Boston Herald, July, 1930.

Boston Post, July, 1930.

‡*Narodna Vola*, Scranton, 1912–34.

‡*Narodne Slovo*, Pittsburgh, 1912–34.

‡*Svoboda*, Jersey City, 1899–1934.

‡*Ukrainia*, Chicago, 1931.

‡ The papers indicated by a double dagger are in Ukrainian. The most important to the student of history is the *Svoboda*.

INDEX

Adam, Bishop, 106

Agents, Jewish steamship, 17; *see also* Steamship agents

Agricultural communities: list of, 57–58; settlements of: in New England, 47; in New Jersey, 49; in New York, 48; in Oklahoma and Texas, 51–52

Agriculture, contribution to, 46 ff.

Alaska Herald and Svoboda, 111

America established, 102, 111

American dollars sent to Ukraine by emigrants, 16

American Legion, Ukrainian membership in, 132

American letters to the Ukraine: influence of, 15–16; theft of, 16

American money, value of, in Austria and Russia, 13

American newspapers in Ukrainian homes, 121

American Russian Falcon, 79

Americanization classes, 131

Amerikansky Russky Viestnik, 79, 115, 119

Andruchovich, Rev. Fr., 111

Antireligious propaganda, 108

Archipenko, Alexander, 71–72, 75; exhibition of work of, 142

Ardan, Ivan, 99, 106, 113; on Ukrainian farms in East Galicia, 14

Art exhibits, 141–42

Athletes, professional, 34

Athletics, participation in, 130

Austria, practice of playing one nationality against another, 6

Austrian government: attempts to stop emigration, 18; frees serfs in 1848, 14

Avramenko, Vasile, 89–90; 139

Avramenko's schools of folk dancing, 88–90; 135–36

Balch, Emily, on farms in Ukraine, 14

Bakeries, 63, 65–66

Banking business, 67, 74 (n. 32)

Barabash, Captain John, 70

Baseball, 130

Basketball, 130

Batu, Mongolian invasion of Ukraine by, 2–3

Benetzky, George, 138

Benevolent societies, 77; benefits of, to members, 81–82; conventions of, 81; early restrictions of, 81; effect of depression upon, 83; government of, 81; philanthropic work of, 82; pro-Russian faction of, 79; scholarships provided by, 82

Bohachevsky, Bishop Constantin, 23, 103, 126, 129

Bohdan, Bishop, 106

Bonchevsky, Antin, 22, 99, 106, 112

Bortniansky, 5

Boston Tercentenary, Ukrainian participation in, 135

Building and loan associations, 67

Bukovoy, Alexey, 56

Bukovoy, Wasyl, 65

Bychinsky, Z., 106

Canada, Ukrainian writers of, 120

Catholics (Uniates), 97, 104

Centers of Ukrainian population, 33

Chandoha, M., 113

Chicago chorus, 136–38; participation of, in music festivals, 138–39

Choruses, 136–38

Christianity, adoption of, in Ukraine, 2, 95

Church: attendance of, 107–8; building era of, 99–101; choir leaders (*diaks*) of, 69, 127; choirs, 133, 135–36; dramatic clubs, 126; factions, 76; government, 101; as influential unit of society, 76; lawsuits of, 101–3; membership of, 104–6; number of, 105–6; parish libraries, 107, 144; philanthropic organizations, 104; relations with the press, 102, 114, 116, 117; schools, 104, 126; sects, 105–6; social functions of, 107

Chutro, Dimitry, 75 (n. 45), 140

Chylak, George, 132

Chyz, Yaroslav, 113